My First Question and Answer Book

First published in 2017 by Miles Kelly Publishing Ltd
Harding's Barn, Bardfield End Green, Thaxted, Essex, CM6 3PX, UK

2 4 6 8 10 9 7 5 3 1

Publishing Director **Belinda Gallagher**
Creative Director **Jo Cowan**
Editorial Assistant **Carly Blake**
Cover Designer **Jo Cowan**
Designers **Jo Cowan, Venita Kidwai, Sophie Pelham, Elaine Wilkinson, Candice Bekir**
Indexer **Helen Snaith**
Production **Elizabeth Collins, Caroline Kelly**
Reprographics **Stephan Davis, Jennifer Cozens, Thom Allaway, Liberty Newton, Anthony Cambray**
Assets **Lorraine King**

Authors **Camilla de la Bedoyere, Catherine Chambers, Chris Oxlade**

ISBN 978-1-78617-331-7

Printed in China

British Library Cataloguing-in-Publication Data
A catalogue record for this book is available from the British Library

Made with paper from a sustainable forest

www.mileskelly.net

My First Question and Answer Book

Miles Kelly

Contents

Questions about...

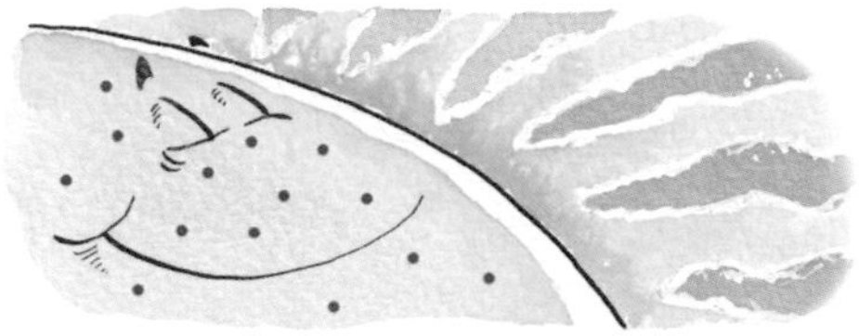

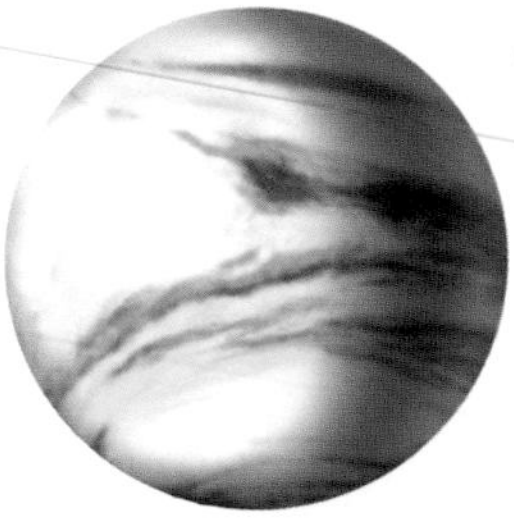

Space

Which star keeps us warm?

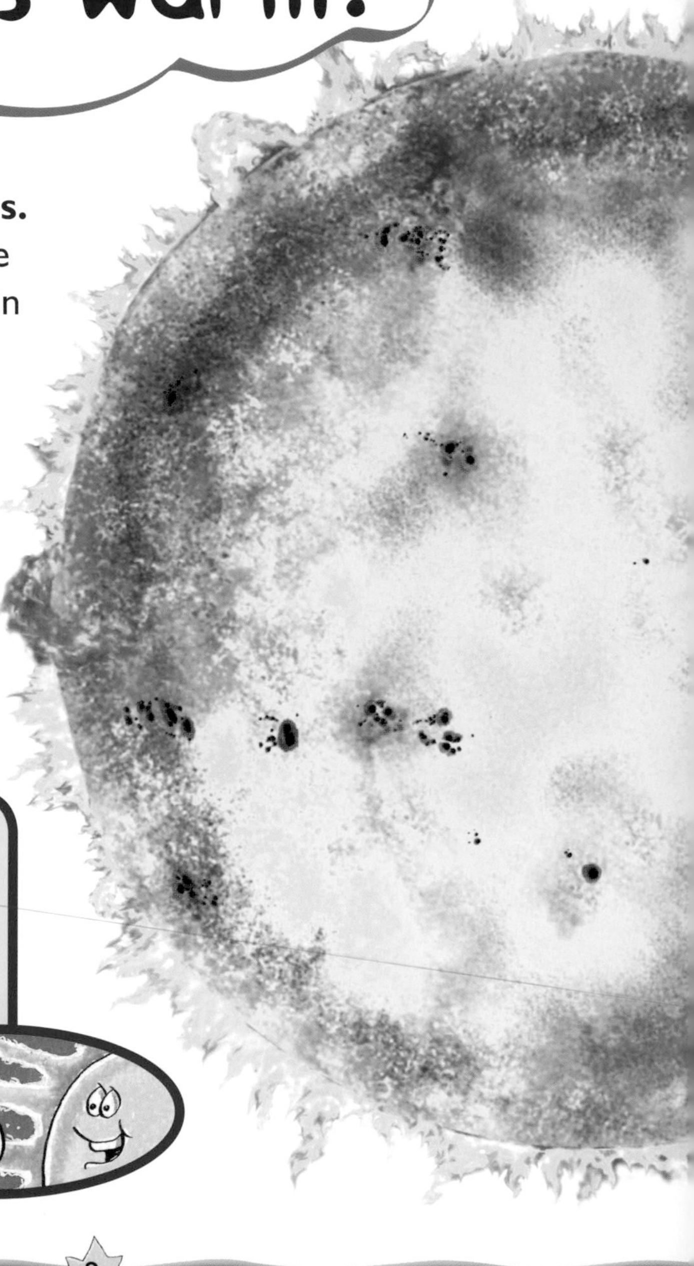

The Sun does. It is a star like all the others in the night sky, but it is much closer to Earth. The Sun is a giant ball of hot, glowing gas and it gives off heat that keeps the Earth warm. It also gives us light.

Hot hot hot!

The Sun's surface is so hot that it would melt a metal spacecraft flying near it! It is 60 times hotter than boiling water.

When is it night time during the day?

Sometimes the Sun, the Earth and the Moon all line up in space. When this happens, the Moon's shadow falls on the Earth, making it dark even if it's daytime. This is called an eclipse.

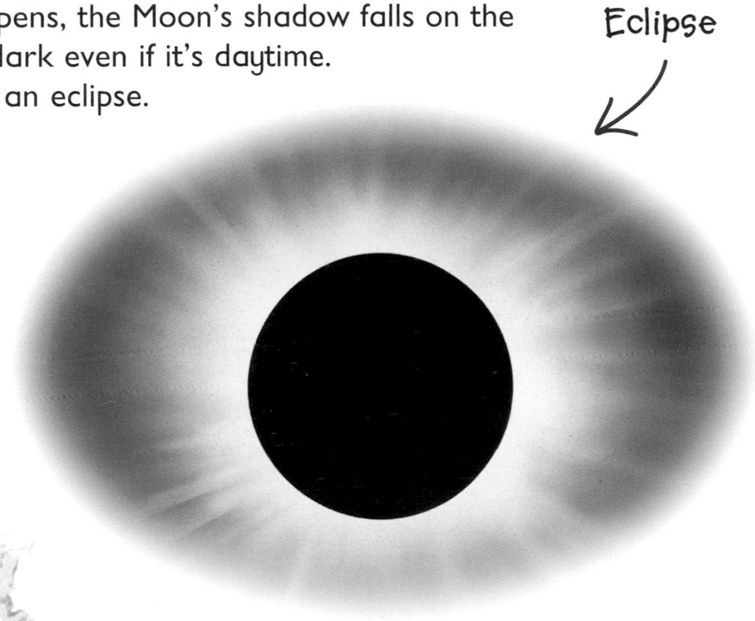

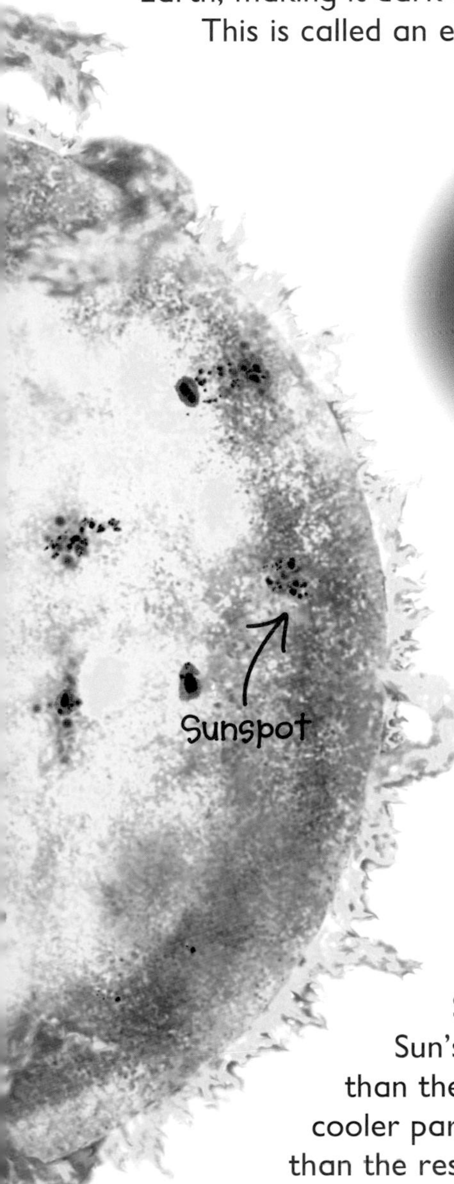

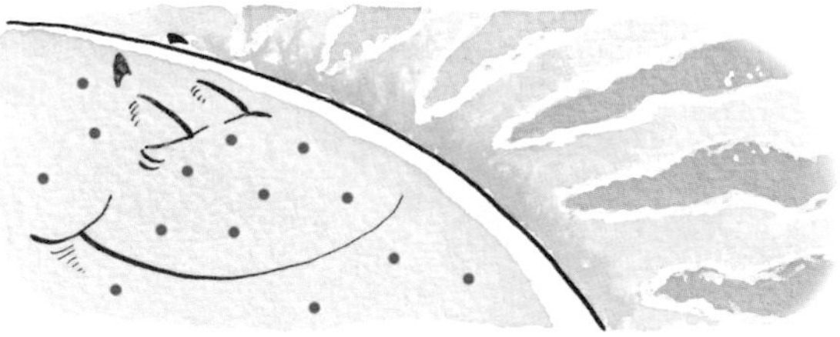

Why is the Sun spotty?

Some parts of the Sun's surface are cooler than the rest of it. These cooler parts appear darker than the rest of the Sun, like spots on its surface. They are called sunspots.

Remember

Never look straight at the Sun. Your eyes could be badly damaged.

Is Earth the only planet near the Sun?

No, there are other planets near the Sun. Mercury and Venus are nearer to the Sun than the Earth is. The other planets are further away. All the planets move around the Sun in huge circles. The Sun and its family of planets is called the Solar System.

Draw

Can you draw a picture of all the planets? You could copy the pictures on this page.

Do other planets have moons?

Earth is not the only planet with a moon. Mars has two moons. Jupiter and Saturn have more than 30 moons each. Venus and Mercury are the only planets with no moons.

What are the other planets like?

Mercury, Venus and Mars are rocky planets, like the Earth. They have solid surfaces. Jupiter, Saturn, Uranus and Neptune are balls of gas and liquid. They are much bigger than the rocky planets. Pluto is a dwarf planet.

One big, happy family!

There are millions of smaller members in the Sun's family. Tiny specks of dust speed between the planets along with chunks of rock called asteroids.

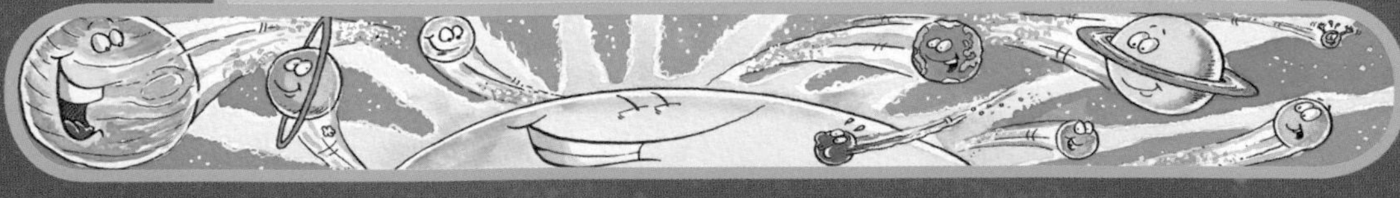

What is inside the Earth?

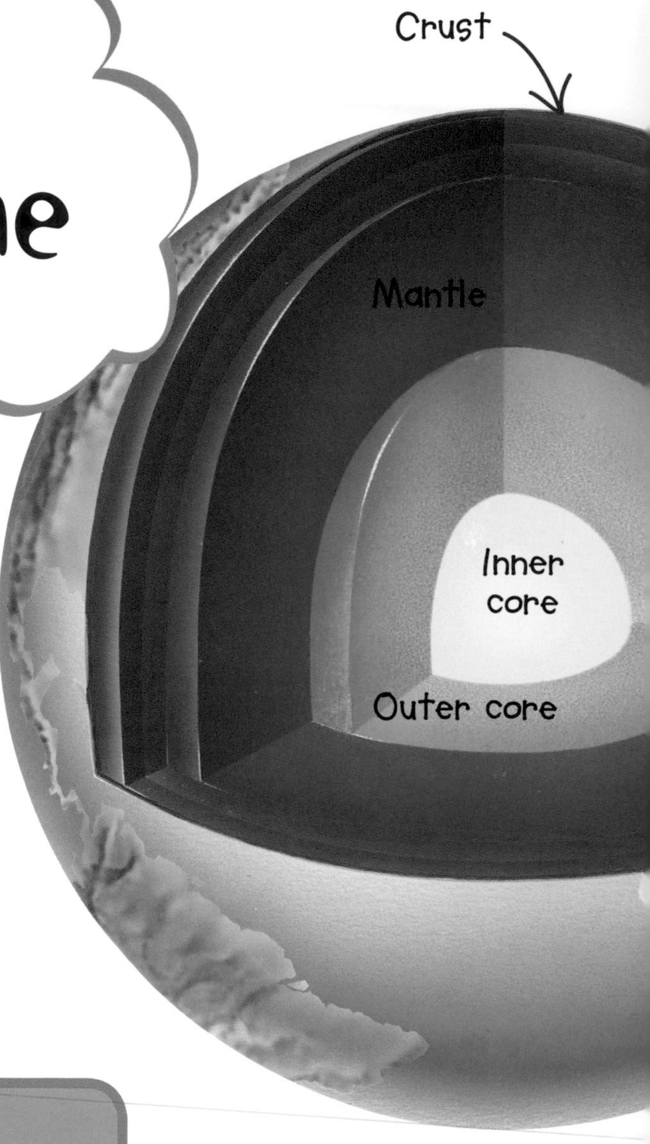

There are layers of hot rock inside the Earth. We live on the Earth's surface where the rock is solid. Beneath the surface, the rock is hot. In some places, it has melted. This melted rock may leak from a volcano.

Living it up!

Earth is the only planet with water on its surface. This means that people, plants and animals can live here. No life has yet been found on other planets.

New Moon | Crescent Moon | First quarter Moon | Gibbous Moon | Full Moon

Why does the Moon change shape?

The Sun lights up one side of the Moon. The other side is dark. As the Moon circles the Earth, we see different parts of the lit side. This is why the Moon seems to change shape.

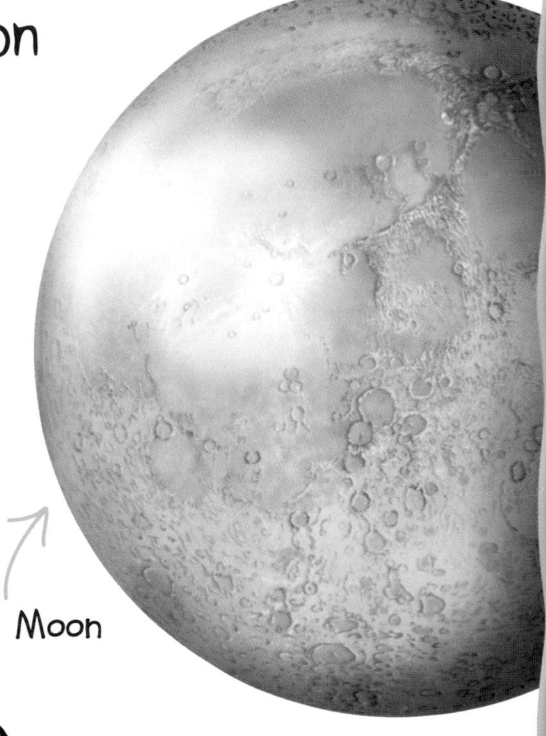

The Moon

Why do we have day and night?

The Earth spins round once every day. When the part you live on faces the Sun, it is daytime. When this part faces away from the Sun, the sunlight can't reach you. Then it is night time.

Look

Look at the picture of the Moon. The circles are called craters. They were made by lumps of rock smashing into the Moon's surface.

What is the hottest planet?

Venus is the hottest planet in the Solar System. Its surface is hotter than the inside of an oven. Venus is covered in a blanket of thick, yellow gas. The gases trap heat from the Sun but don't let it escape. This means that Venus can't cool down.

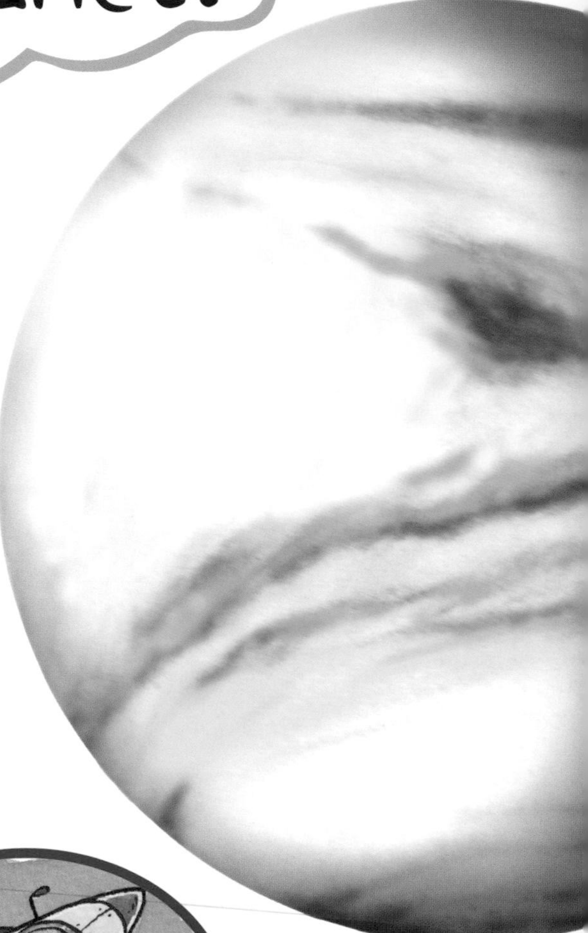

Venus

Back in a year!

Nobody has ever been to Mars. It is so far away that it would take a spacecraft six months to get there. It would take another six months to get home again!

Why is Mars called the red planet?

Mars looks red because it is covered with red rocks and red dust, the colour of rust. Sometimes, winds pick up the dust and make swirling dust storms. In 1971 dust storms covered the whole planet. The surface completely disappeared from view!

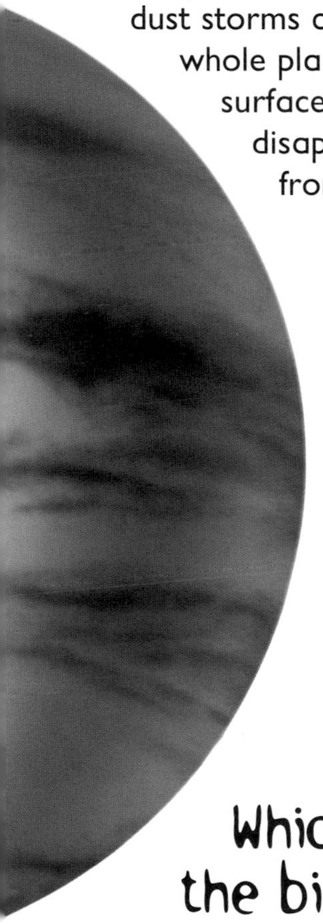

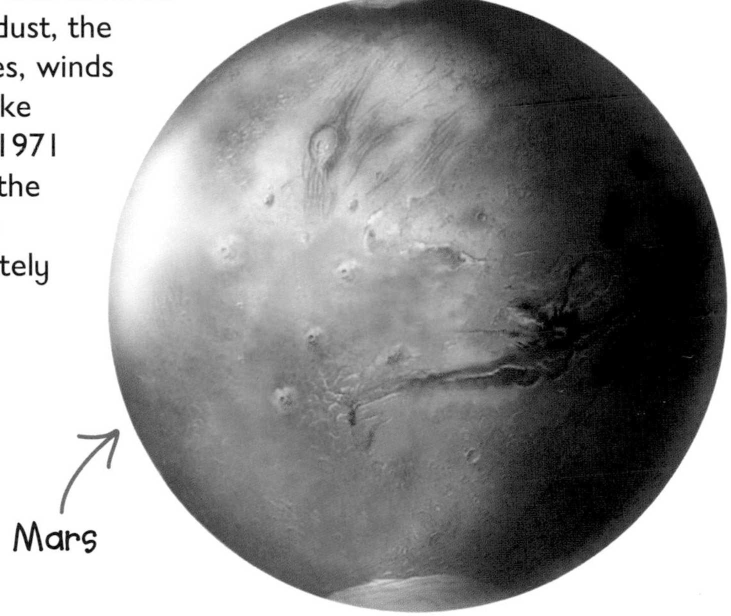

Which planet has the biggest volcano?

Mars has the biggest volcano. It is called Olympus Mons and it is three times higher than Mount Everest, the highest mountain on Earth. Olympus Mons has gently sloping sides, like an upside-down plate. Mars has many other volcanoes, too. There are also giant canyons and craters.

Discover

Try looking for Venus in the night sky. It looks like a bright star in the early morning or evening.

Does Pluto have its own moon?

Yes, it does. Pluto, a dwarf planet, has its own moon called Charon. Charon is half the size of Pluto and was discovered by scientists in 1978. It takes Charon six and a half Earth days to orbit around Pluto.

Why does Mercury look like the Moon?

Mercury looks a bit like our Moon. It is covered in dents called craters. These were made when rocks crashed into the surface. There is no wind or rain on Mercury, or the Moon, to wear away the craters.

Sun trap!

Mercury is very close to the Sun. It gets much hotter there than on Earth. If you travelled to Mercury, you would need a special spacesuit and shoes to protect you from the heat.

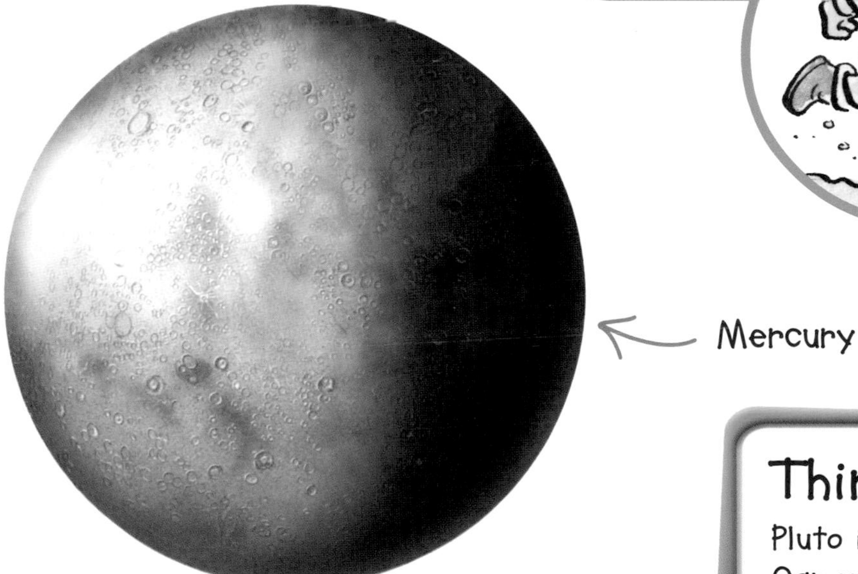

Think

Pluto is really cold. Can you think why?

Which planet is baking hot and freezing cold?

Mercury is hot and cold. It spins very slowly. The side that faces the Sun is baked until it is hotter than the inside of an oven. When this side faces away from the Sun, it cools down until it is colder than a freezer.

What is the biggest planet?

Jupiter is the biggest planet. It is 11 times as wide as the Earth. All the other planets in the Solar System would fit inside it! Jupiter is covered in swirls of red and orange gas. These are giant storms.

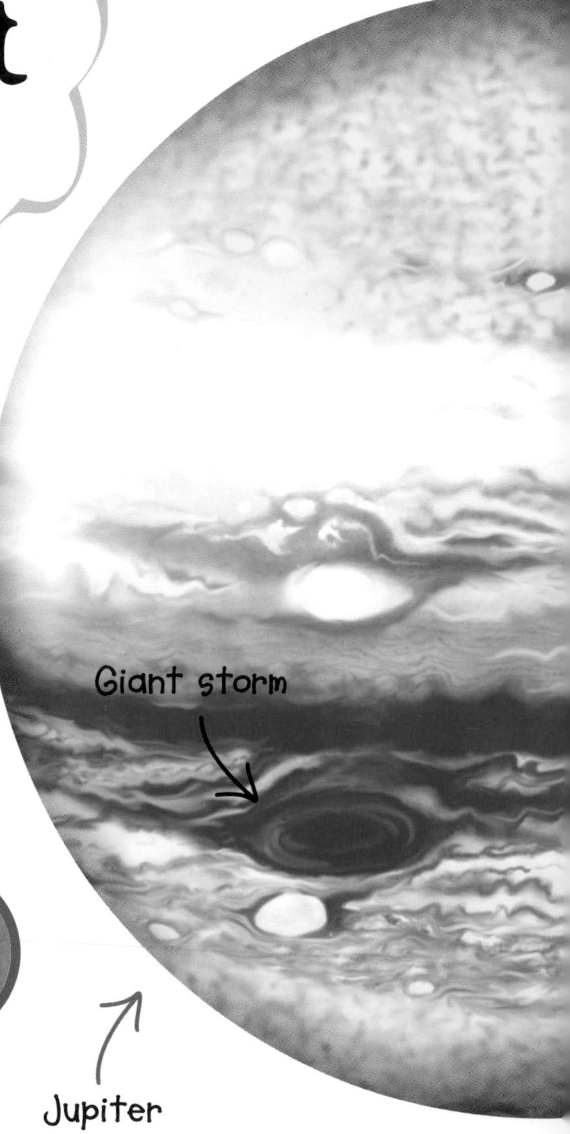

Moon pizza!

Io is one of Jupiter's moons. It is covered in yellow and orange blotches. Io looks like a pizza in space! The blotches are made by hot liquid that comes out of volcanoes.

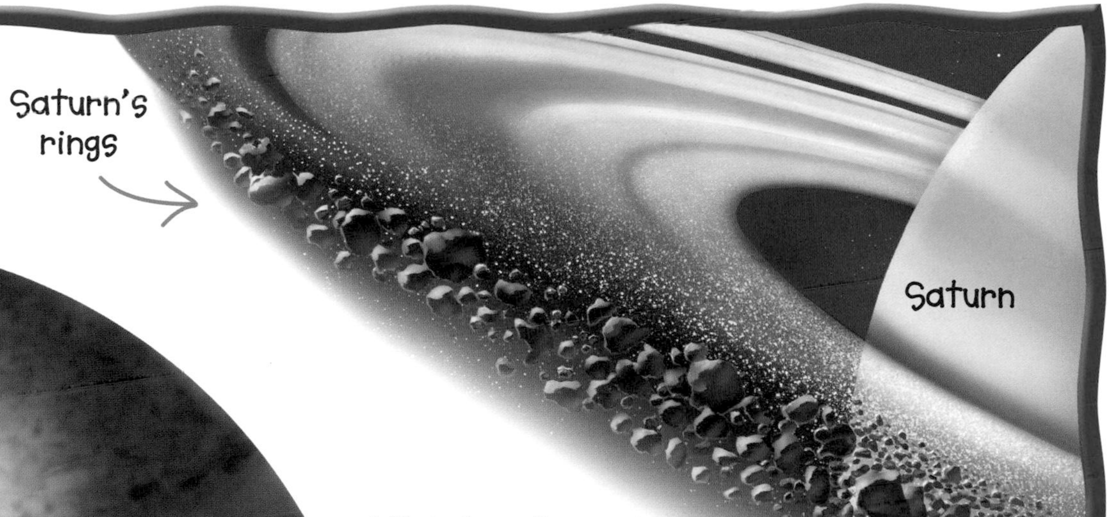

Which planet has rings?

Saturn is surrounded by rings that shine brightly in the sunlight. The rings are made from millions and millions of lumps of ice. Some lumps are the size of ice cubes. Others are as big as cars!

Count

Can you count how many planet Earths there are on these pages?

Is there a giant made of gas?

Not really! However, Jupiter and Saturn are called gas giants. This is because they don't have solid surfaces like the Earth. They have a thick layer of gas and then liquid. You couldn't land on them in a spacecraft.

Which planet rolls around?

Uranus is different to the other planets. Most planets are almost upright. They spin as they move around the Sun. Uranus is tipped right over on its side. This planet spins, too, but it looks as though it is rolling around!

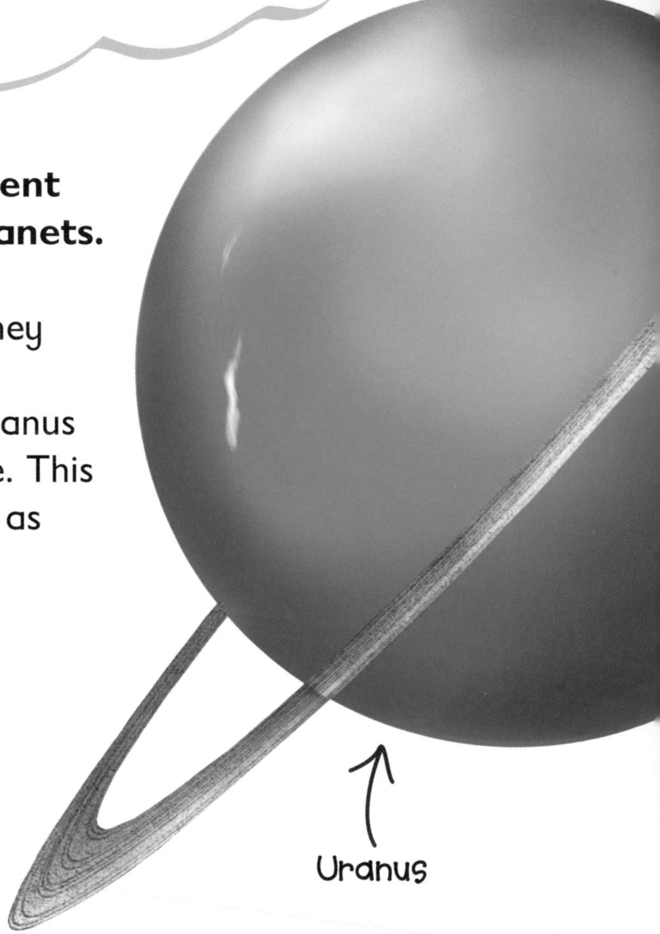

New new moons!

Astronomers (scientists that study space) keep finding new moons around Uranus. They have found 27 so far. There are four big moons and lots of small ones. But there may be more!

Why does Neptune look so blue?

Neptune is covered in bright blue clouds. Sometimes there are streaky, icy white clouds, too. One white cloud is called The Scooter because it scoots around Neptune at high speed. There is also a giant storm called the Great Dark Spot.

Why do Neptune and Pluto swap places?

Most of the planets move around the Sun in huge circles. Pluto's circle is a bit squashed. This means that it is sometimes closer to the Sun than Neptune. Then it is Neptune's turn to be the planet that is furthest from the Sun!

Remember

Uranus and Neptune have rings. Which other two planets have rings, too?

Are there snowballs in space?

Not really! However, comets are a bit like giant snowballs. They are made up of dust and ice mixed together. When a comet gets close to the Sun, the ice begins to melt. Then dust and gas stream away from the comet. They form a long, bright tail.

What is a shooting star?

A shooting star is a bright streak across the night sky. It is not really a star. It is made when a small lump of rock shoots into the air above the Earth. Because the rock is going so fast, it burns brightly.

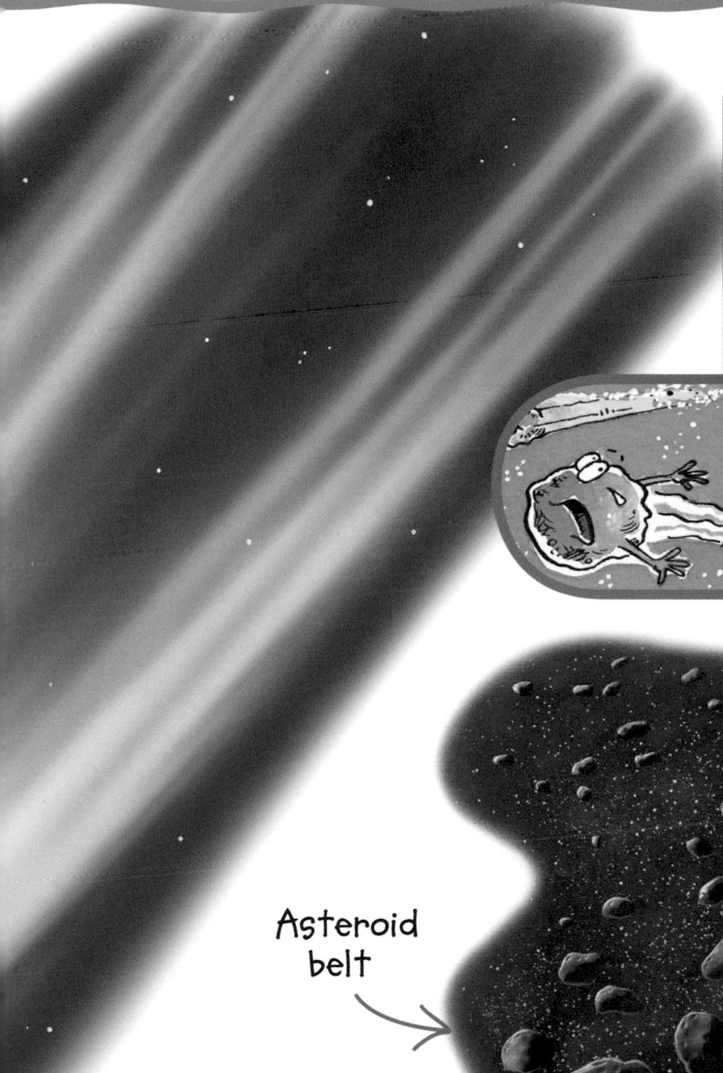

Rocky road!

There are millions of asteroids in the Solar System. Some asteroids are tiny, but some are as big as mountains.

Asteroid belt

Does the Sun have a belt?

The Sun has a belt made up of lumps of rock called asteroids. We call this the asteroid belt. The asteroids move around the Sun between Mars and Jupiter. The biggest asteroids are round, but most are shaped like giant potatoes.

Discover

Can you find out the name of a famous comet?

How are stars made?

Stars are made from huge clouds of dust and gas. Gradually the cloud shrinks and all the gas and dust clump together. The centre of the cloud gets hotter and hotter and a new star begins to shine. The star gives off heat and light.

Shine on!

Stars can shine for thousands of millions of years! The Sun started shining five thousand million years ago. It will stop shining in another five thousand million years.

What is a group of stars called?

A group of stars is called a star cluster. A star cluster is made from a giant cloud of gas and dust. Some clusters contain just a few stars. Others contain hundreds of stars and they look like a big ball of light.

Star cluster

2. The cloud begins to spin

Are all stars white?

Only the most giant stars shine with a bright white light. This is because they are extremely hot. Smaller stars, such as our Sun, are not so hot. They look yellow instead. Very small stars are cooler still. They look red or brown.

Draw

Can you paint white, yellow and red stars on a sheet of black paper?

What is the Milky Way?

The stars in space are in huge groups called galaxies. Our galaxy is called the Milky Way. All the stars in the night sky are in the Milky Way. There are so many that you couldn't count them all in your whole lifetime!

Can galaxies crash?

Sometimes two galaxies crash into each other. But there is no giant bump. This is because galaxies are mostly made of empty space! The stars just go past each other. Galaxies can pull each other out of shape.

Count

Look at the pictures on these pages. How many different shapes of galaxies can you find?

The Milky Way

Elliptical galaxy

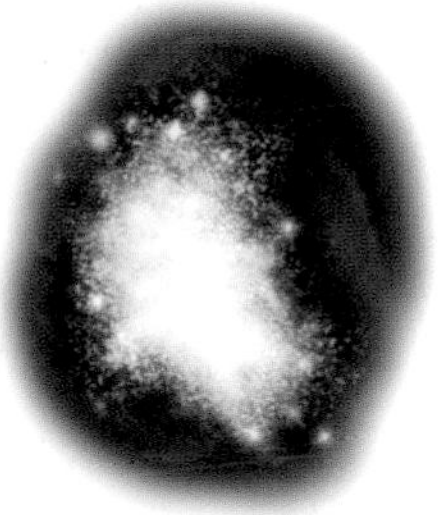

Irregular galaxy

Spiral galaxy

Do galaxies have arms?

Some galaxies have arms that curl in a spiral, like the Milky Way. Other galaxies, called elliptical galaxies, have a round, squashed shape. Many galaxies have no shape and are called irregular galaxies.

Great galaxies!

There are thousands of millions of galaxies in space. Some are much smaller than the Milky Way. Others are much larger. They all contain too many stars to count!

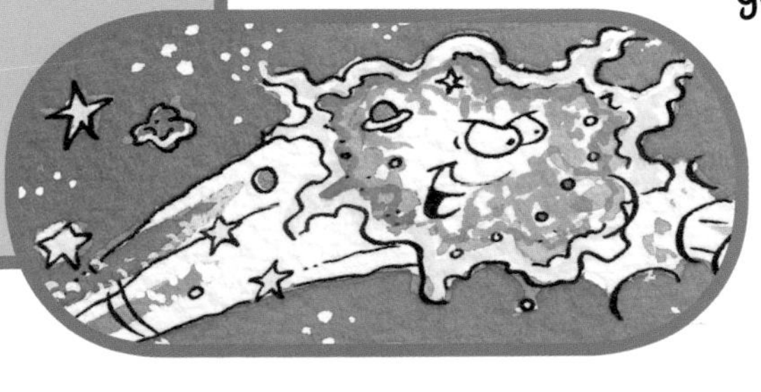

How did shuttles get into space?

Shuttles were reusable manned spacecraft that blasted into space like big rockets. Each shuttle was powered by rocket motors in its tail, fuel from a giant fuel tank, and two booster rockets. The fuel tank and the booster rockets fell off before the shuttle reached space.

Rocket power!

Rockets are filled with fuel. The fuel burns in the rocket motor to make hot gases. The gases rush out of the motor and push the rocket upwards.

How fast do rockets go?

Very, very fast indeed! After blasting off, a rocket goes faster and faster and higher and higher. When it reaches space, it is going 30 times faster than a jumbo jet. If a rocket went slower than this it would fall back to Earth.

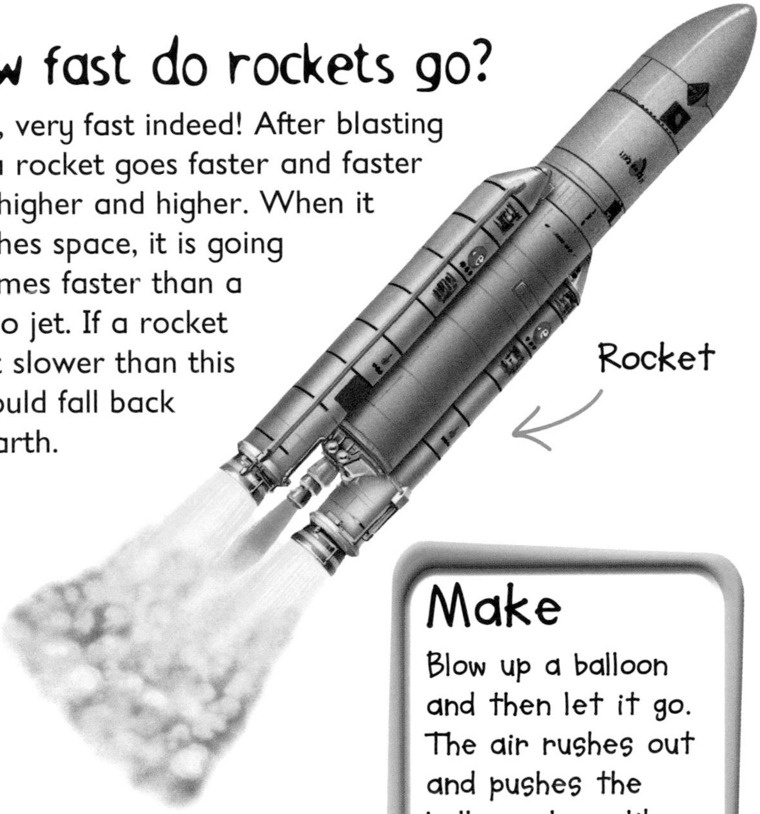

Make

Blow up a balloon and then let it go. The air rushes out and pushes the balloon along, like a simple rocket.

When was a shuttle like a glider?

When a shuttle travelled back to Earth it slowed down, and began to fall. It did not use its motors to fly down – instead, it flew like a giant glider. Then the shuttle landed on a long runway and used a parachute to slow to a stop.

Why do astronauts float in space?

When things are in space they don't have any weight. This means everything floats. So do astronauts! This makes them feel sick, too. In a spacecraft everything is fixed down to stop it floating away. Astronauts have footholds and handholds to grab onto.

All packed?

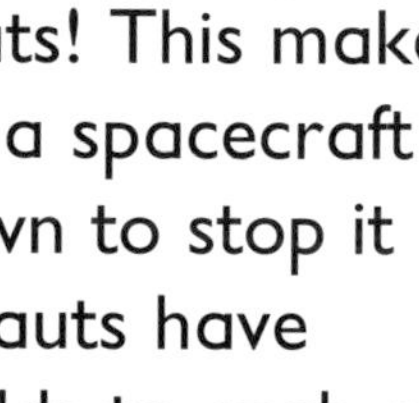

Astronauts must take everything they need into space. In space there is no air, water or food. All of these things have to be packed into the spacecraft and taken into space.

Where do astronauts go to sleep?

Astronauts sleep in sleeping bags. The bags are fixed to the wall inside a spacecraft. They keep astronauts warm and stop them floating about while they sleep! A special shower lets the astronauts wash without drops of water floating everywhere.

Why do astronauts wear spacesuits?

Space is a dangerous place. Spacesuits protect astronauts when they go outside their spacecraft. There is no air in space. So a spacesuit has a supply of air for the astronaut to breathe. The suit also stops an astronaut from getting too hot or too cold.

Remember

Can you remember why astronauts have to carry air with them in space?

Are there robots in space?

There are robot spacecraft, called probes, in space. They have visited all the planets. Some probes travel around the planets. They send photographs and other information back to Earth. Other probes land on a planet to take a closer look.

Snap happy!

A probe called *Voyager 2* was the first to visit Uranus and Neptune. It took photographs of the planets and sent them back to Earth.

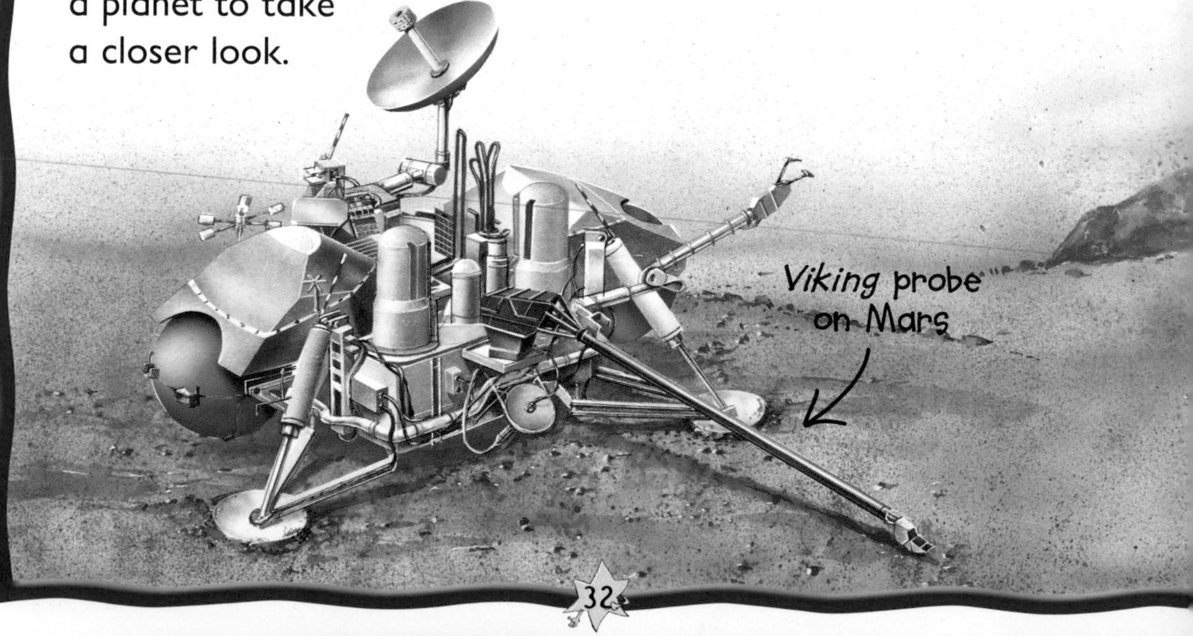

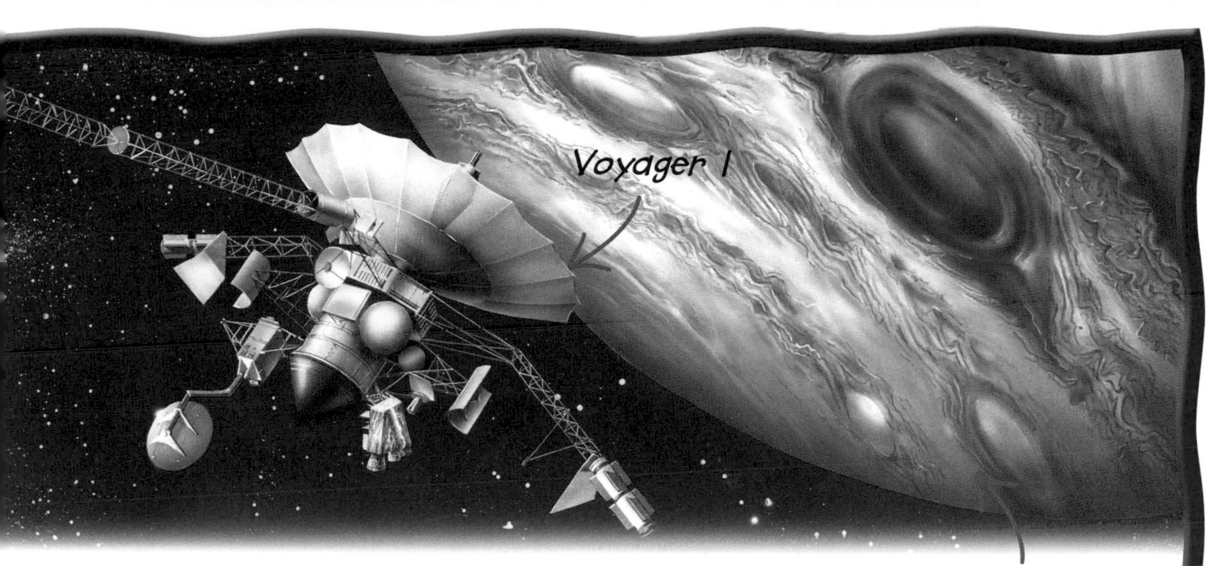

Which probe has travelled the furthest?

A probe called *Voyager 1* was launched from Earth in 1977. It visited Jupiter in 1979 and then Saturn in 1980. Then it kept going, out of the Solar System. *Voyager 1* is now 14 thousand million kilometres from Earth!

Draw

Try designing your own robot explorer. You can take some ideas from these pages.

Have probes been to Mars?

More probes have been to Mars than any other planet. In 1997 a probe called Pathfinder landed on Mars. Inside Pathfinder was a tiny robot vehicle, called *Sojourner*. Scientists steered it using remote control. It investigated the soil and rocks on Mars.

Quiz time

Do you remember what you have read about space?

Here are some questions to test your memory. The pictures will help you. If you get stuck, read the pages again.

1. Which star keeps us warm?

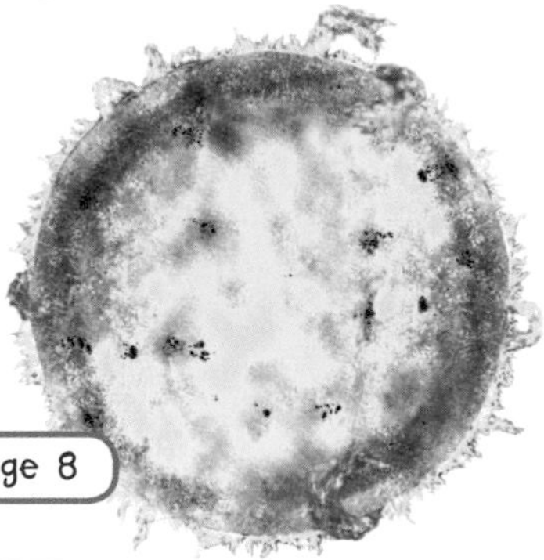

page 8

2. Why is the Sun spotty?

page 9

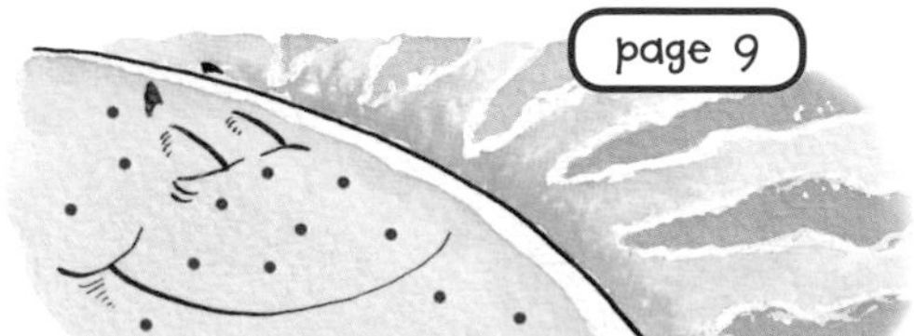

page 14

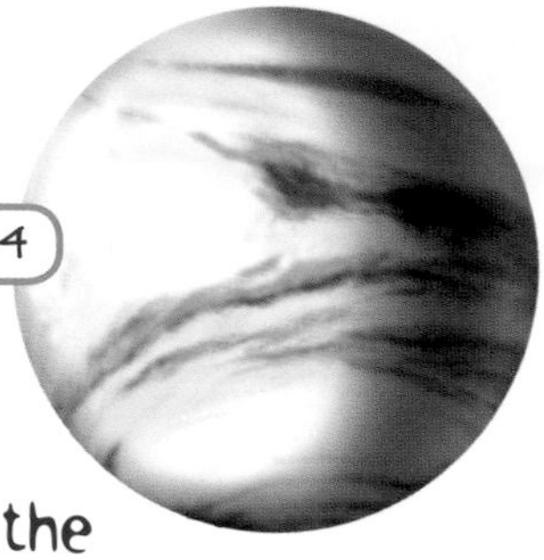

3. What is the hottest planet?

4. Why is Mars called the red planet?

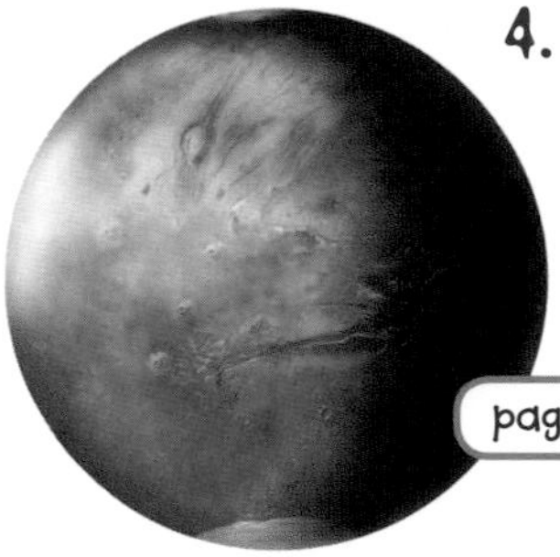

page 15

page 16

5. What is Charon?

page 22

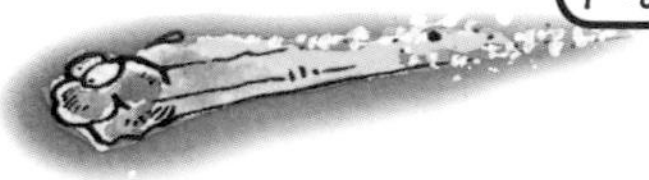

6. What is a shooting star?

7. Does the Sun have a belt?

page 23

11. How did shuttles get into space?

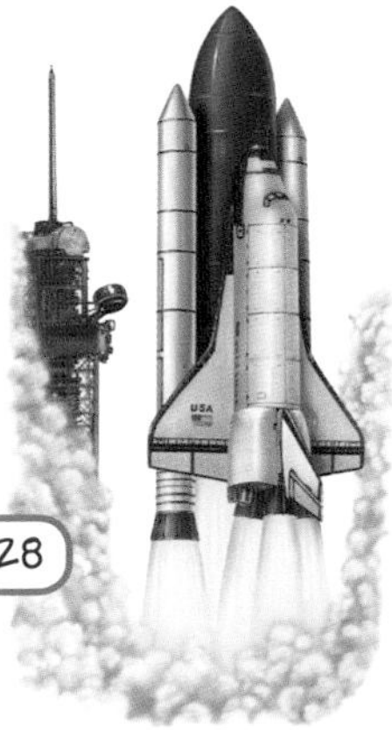

page 28

8. What is a group of stars called?

page 25

12. When was a shuttle like a glider?

page 29

13. Why do astronauts float in space?

page 30

9. What is the Milky Way?

page 26

10. Can galaxies crash?

page 26

Answers

1. The Sun
2. Cooler parts look darker, like spots
3. Venus
4. It is covered with red rocks and dust
5. Pluto's moon
6. A lump of rock burning in the sky
7. Yes, the asteroid belt
8. Star cluster
9. A huge group of stars
10. Yes
11. Like a giant rocket does
12. When it travelled back to Earth
13. Because they have no weight in space

Questions about...

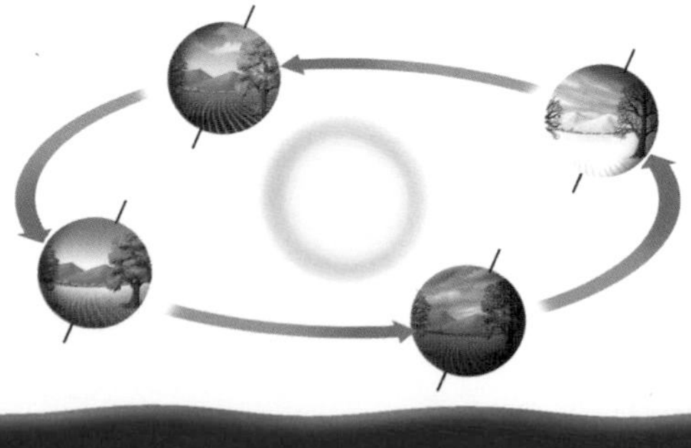

Weather

Why is summer warm and sunny?

The Earth is tipped to one side as it moves round the Sun. Some of the year, the north half of the Earth faces the Sun. Then the Sun is higher in the sky, making the weather warm. This is summer. When the southern half of the Earth faces the Sun, it is winter in the north.

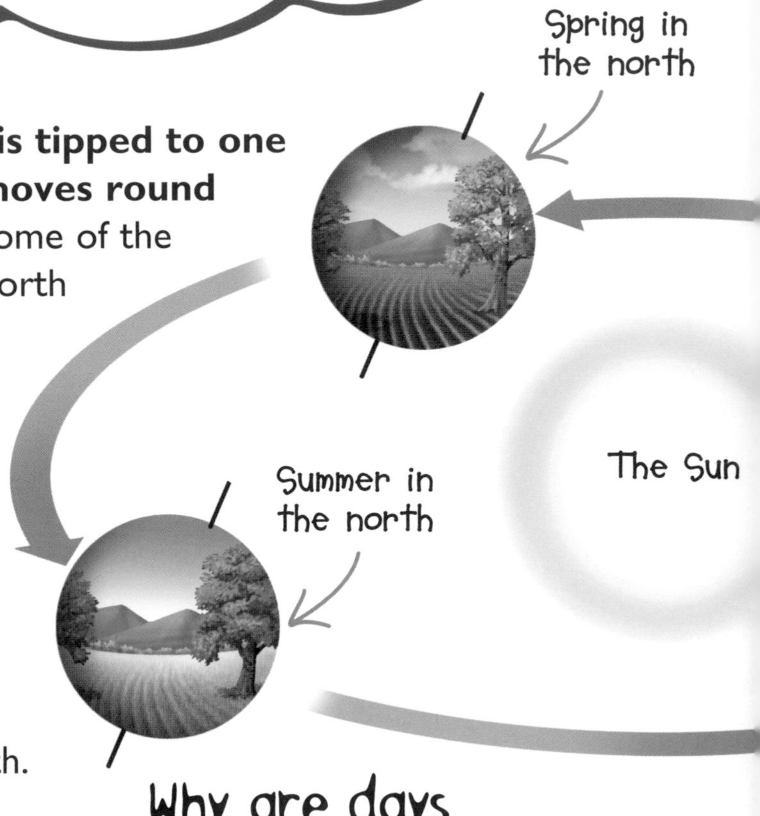

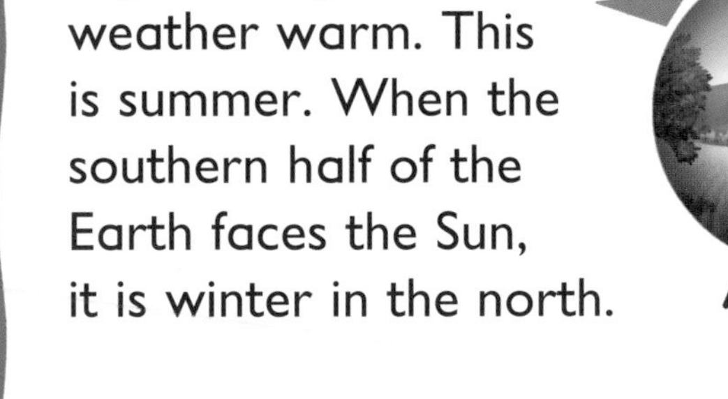

Why are days longer in summer?

Summer days are longer because the Earth is tilted and spins round. In summer, the Sun rises earlier and sets later. This makes daytime last longer than night. In the middle of summer in Sweden it is light for 21 hours!

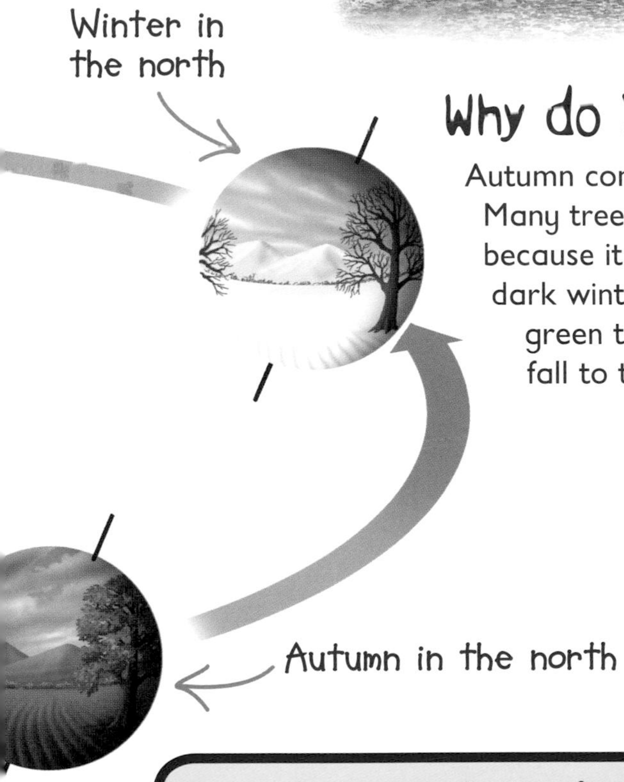

Why do leaves fall in autumn?

Autumn comes between summer and winter. Many trees lose their leaves in autumn because it is hard for them to grow in the dark winter months. The leaves turn from green to red, orange or brown. Then they fall to the ground.

Find

Can you find photographs of red, orange and brown leaves in autumn?

Sunshine at midnight!

At the North and South Poles, the Sun never sets in summer. It is light all day. In winter, the Sun never rises. Then it is dark all day long!

What is the sunniest place?

The Sahara Desert in North Africa is the sunniest place on Earth. It is sunny for nearly 12 hours every day! It hardly rains, which makes it hard for plants and animals to live here. People dress in loose clothes to stop being sunburnt.

Sea makes fire!

El Niño is a warm water current (a big stream) in the Pacific Ocean. Scientists think that this could cause droughts. Some extreme droughts can lead to forest fires.

When is a lake not a lake?

When it's a mirage! A mirage often happens on a hot day. Hot air near the ground makes light from the bright sky bend upwards. This makes it seem as if there is a lake on the ground in the distance. Really the ground is dry!

People living in the desert

Remember

Can you remember why desert people wear loose clothes, even when it is very hot?

Drought

What happens when it doesn't rain?

Sometimes it is dry for a long time in places where it normally rains a lot. This is called a drought. There was a drought in the United States in the 1930s. Crops didn't grow and fields turned to dust. Many people had to leave their farms.

Does Earth have a blanket?

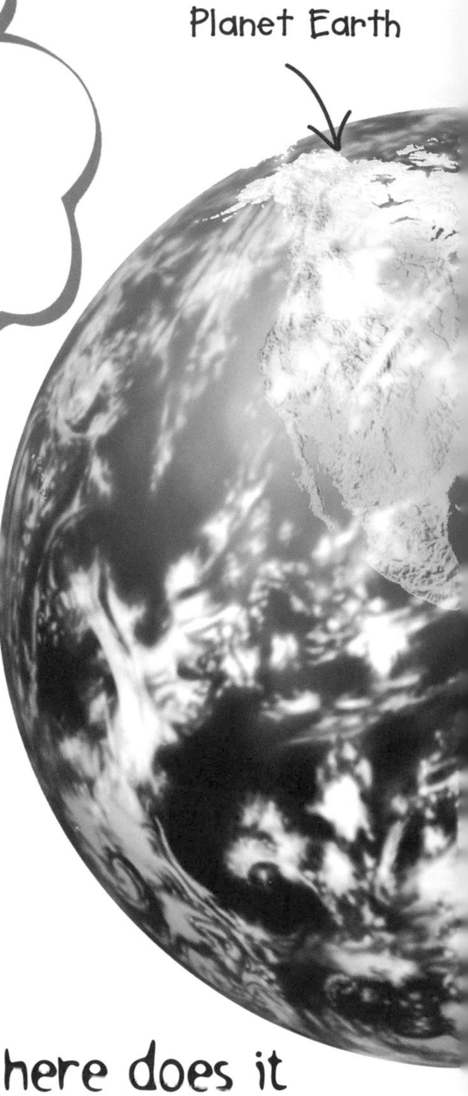

Yes, it does. The Earth is wrapped in a thick blanket of air. It is called the atmosphere. This is where all the weather happens. The atmosphere also helps to keep the Earth's surface warm at night. In the day it protects us from harmful rays coming from the Sun.

Where does it rain every day?

In a tropical rainforest the weather is always very hot and very wet. The Sun shines every day, and there are downpours of heavy rain, too. Rainforest plants grow very quickly in this steamy weather.

Monsoon downpour!

In some countries it pours with rain for a few weeks every year. This is called a monsoon. In India, enough rain falls in one year to cover the ground with water 26 metres deep!

How deep is the atmosphere?

The atmosphere stretches hundreds of kilometres above our heads. If you go up through the atmosphere, the air gets thinner and thinner. High up in mountains, mountaineers find it difficult to breathe so they take breathing equipment with them.

Mountaineer

Look

Look at the picture of the Earth above. What do you think the white swirly patterns are?

Where does rain come from?

Most rain comes from the sea! Some seawater turns to gas in the air. If the air rises, the gas becomes water drops. These make clouds. If the drops get big enough, they fall as rain. The water flows back to the sea.

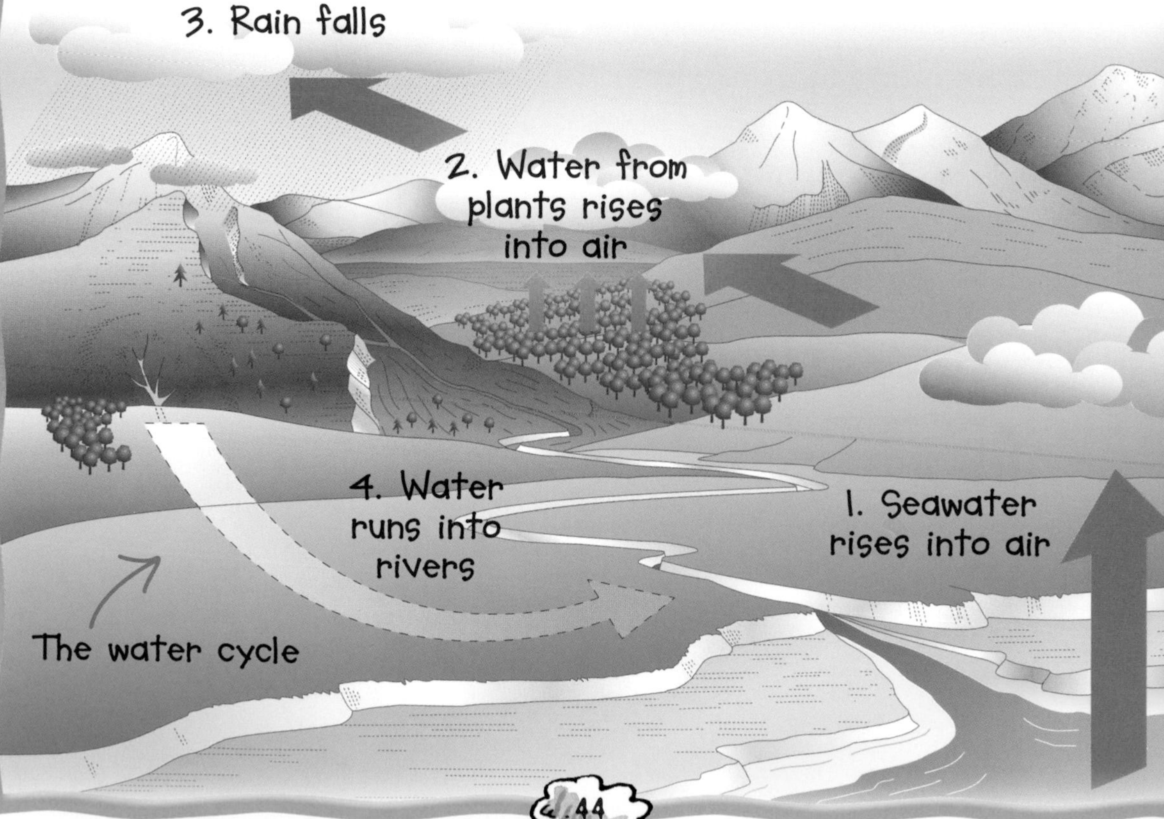

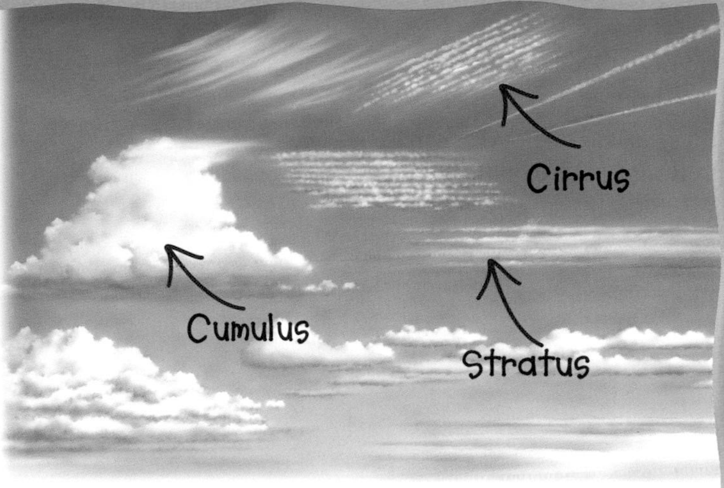

Head in the clouds!

The tops of tall mountains are often in the clouds. At the top it looks misty. Mountaineers sometimes get lost in these clouds!

Are all clouds small and fluffy?

Clouds come in lots of different shapes and sizes. Weather experts give the different clouds names. Fluffy clouds are called cumulus clouds. Some are small and some are giant. Flat clouds are called stratus clouds. Wispy clouds high in the sky are called cirrus clouds.

What rain never lands?

Sometimes rain that falls from a cloud never reaches the ground. If the drops of rain fall into very dry air, the water in them turns into gas. This means that the drops disappear and never reach the ground.

Look

Look at the clouds outside today. Are they fluffy or flat? The picture above will help you.

What happens in a flood?

Sometimes a lot of rain falls in a few hours. So much water flows into rivers that they fill up and burst their banks. The rivers flood the land on each side. Sometimes houses disappear under the flood water.

Floods of tears!

The river Nile in Egypt floods every year. Thousands of years ago, the Egyptians made up a story about the flood. It said that a goddess called Isis cried so much that the river filled up with her tears.

Did Noah build an ark?

The Bible tells the story of a man called Noah. He built a great boat called an ark to escape a flood. We don't know if Noah's ark existed. Scientists have found out that there probably was a huge flood thousands of years ago.

Noah's ark

Flooded house

Find

Can you find the country of Egypt and the river Nile in an atlas?

Can there be a flood in a desert?

Yes there can. Most of the time there is no rain in a desert. The hot Sun bakes the ground hard. Once in a while, it rains heavily. The water flows off the ground instead of soaking in. This can cause a flood.

What is snow made of?

Snow is made of ice, which is water that has frozen. When it is very cold in a cloud, tiny bits of ice (crystals) begin to form, instead of water drops. The pieces clump together to make snowflakes that fall to the ground. The weather must be very cold for snow to fall. If it is too warm, the snowflakes melt and turn to rain.

Shiver!

Antarctica is the coldest place on Earth. The lowest temperature ever recorded there is –89°C. That's much, much colder than inside a freezer!

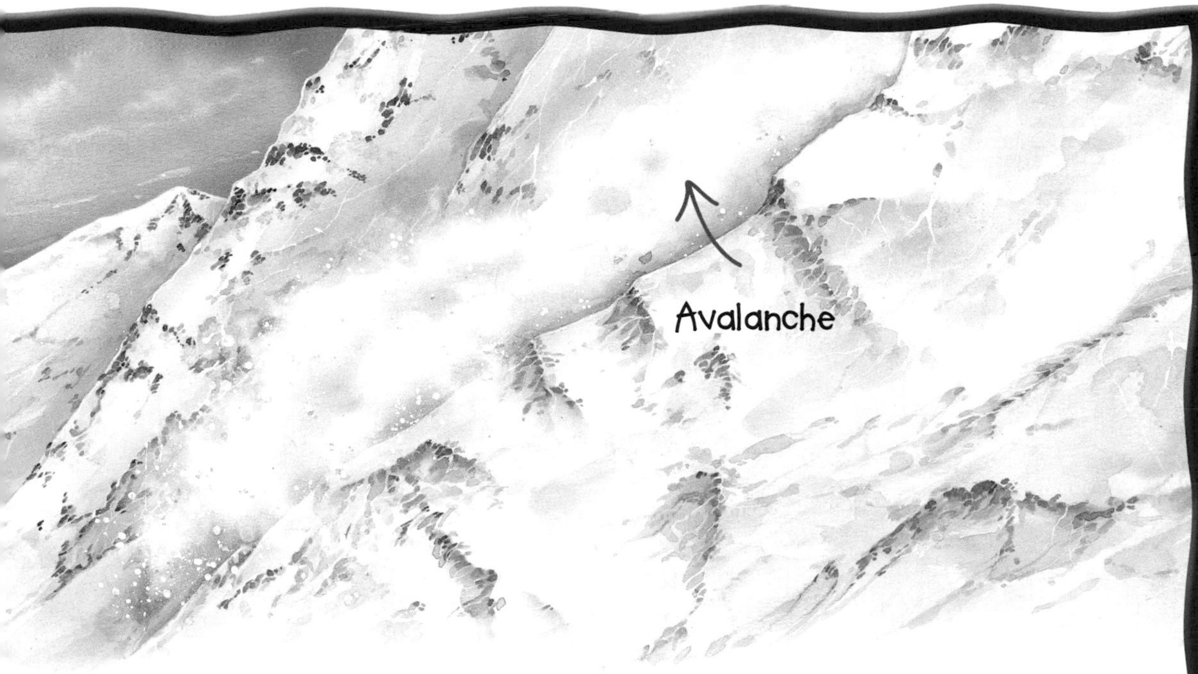

When is snow dangerous?

When lots of snow falls on mountains, deep layers build up on the slopes. The snow may suddenly slide down the mountain. This is an avalanche. A big avalanche can bury a town. A loud noise or even a person walking on the snow can start an avalanche.

Are all snowflakes the same?

It's hard to believe, but all snowflakes are different – even though there are millions and millions of them. This is because every ice crystal in a snowflake has its own shape. No two crystals are the same. Most ice crystals in snowflakes looks like stars with six points.

Think

Can you think why it could be dangerous to ski across a steep hillside covered with snow?

Where are the fastest winds?

Inside a tornado. A tornado is like a spinning funnel made of air. They reach down from giant thunderstorms. The winds can blow at 480 kilometres an hour. That's twice as fast as an express train! Tornadoes can rip trees from the ground and destroy houses.

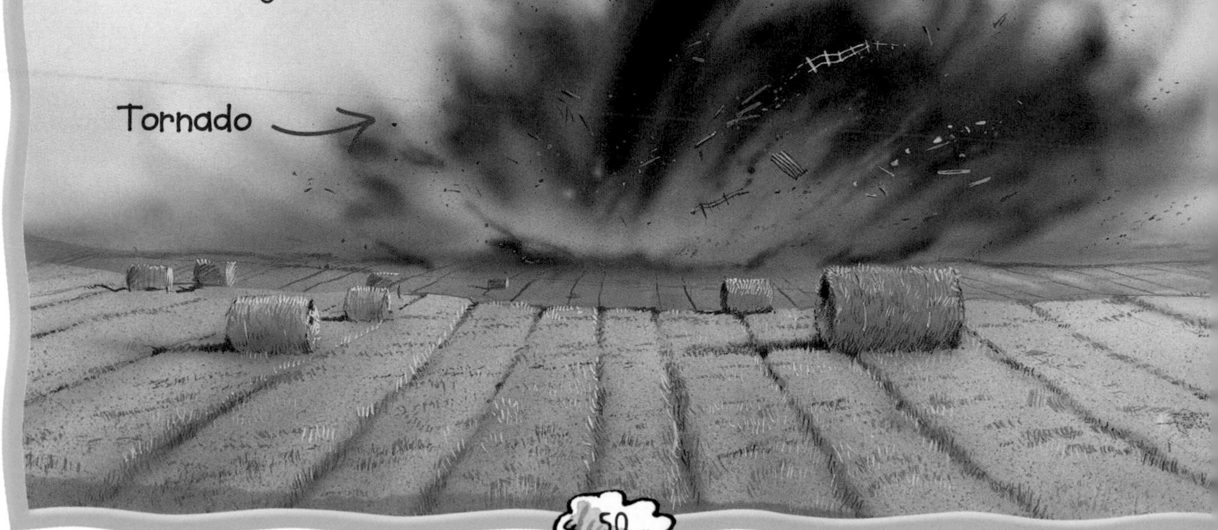

Which storm has an eye?

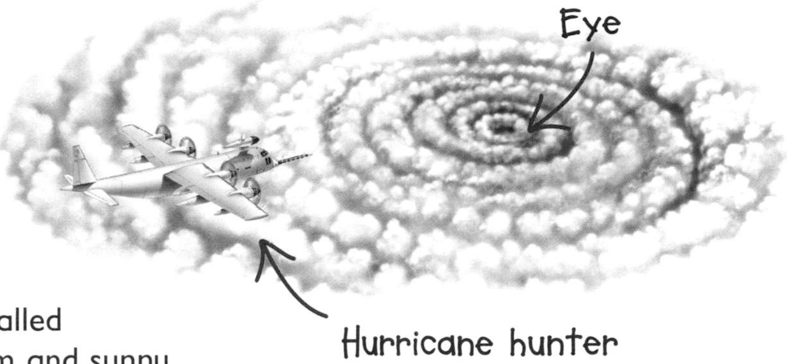

A hurricane is a giant spinning storm made up of super-strong winds. The centre is a hole called the eye. Here it is calm and sunny. If a hurricane reaches land, the winds can damage buildings and heavy rain causes floods. Hurricane hunters are planes that fly into hurricanes to measure the wind speed.

Draw

Look at the pictures on this page. Can you draw a picture of a tornado and a hurricane?

Stormy names!

A tropical storm that starts in the Atlantic Ocean is called a hurricane. In the Pacific Ocean, a tropical storm is called a typhoon. In the Indian Ocean it is called a cyclone.

How do we measure wind?

We measure the wind on a scale called the Beaufort Scale. The slowest wind is Force 1 on the scale. This is called a light breeze. The strongest wind is Force 12. This is called a hurricane. Force zero means there is no wind at all.

What makes the sky clap?

A thunderstorm! Inside a big thundercloud, water drops and bits of ice move up and down, bumping into each other. This makes electricity build up. When the electricity jumps around, we see a spark of lightning and hear a loud clap of thunder.

Huge hail!

Hail is made up of lumps of ice called hailstones. Hail can fall from thunderclouds. The biggest hailstone ever fell in Bangladesh in 1986. It was the size of a grapefruit!

When is lightning like a fork?

When lightning jumps from a thundercloud to the ground, it looks like huge forks in the sky. If lightning jumps from one cloud to another, the clouds light up. This is called sheet lightning.

Lightning can be red, blue, yellow or white.

Lightning

Does lightning hit buildings?

Lightning often hits tall buildings. The buildings have a metal spike on top called a lightning conductor. When lightning hits a building, the lightning conductor carries the electricity to the ground. If there was no lightning conductor, the building could be damaged by the lightning.

Thundercloud

Count

Count the seconds between a flash of lightning and a clap of thunder. The bigger the number, the further away the thunderstorm.

What is a rainbow made of?

A rainbow is made of sunlight. The light bounces through raindrops. This splits the light into different colours. The colours of a rainbow are always the same. They are red, orange, yellow, green, blue, indigo and violet.

Northern lights

Remember

Can you remember all seven colours of a rainbow?

When does the sky have curtains?

In the far north and the far south of the world, amazing patterns of light sometimes appear in the sky. They look like colourful curtains. The patterns are called auroras (or-roar-rers). They happen when tiny light particles from the Sun smash into the air.

Rainbow with no colour!

A fogbow is a rainbow that is white. You might see a fogbow when the Sun shines through fog. It is white because the water drops in fog are too small to split up the light into rainbow colours.

When can you see three suns?

If there are thin clouds high in the sky, you might see three suns. The clouds are made of bits of ice. These bend light from the Sun. This makes it look as if there are two extra suns in the sky. We call these mock suns, or sun dogs.

What is a rain dance?

In many hot places, such as Africa, it only rains once or twice a year.

People may dance traditional rain dances if the rain does not fall. In the past, people believed that rain dances really could bring clouds and rain.

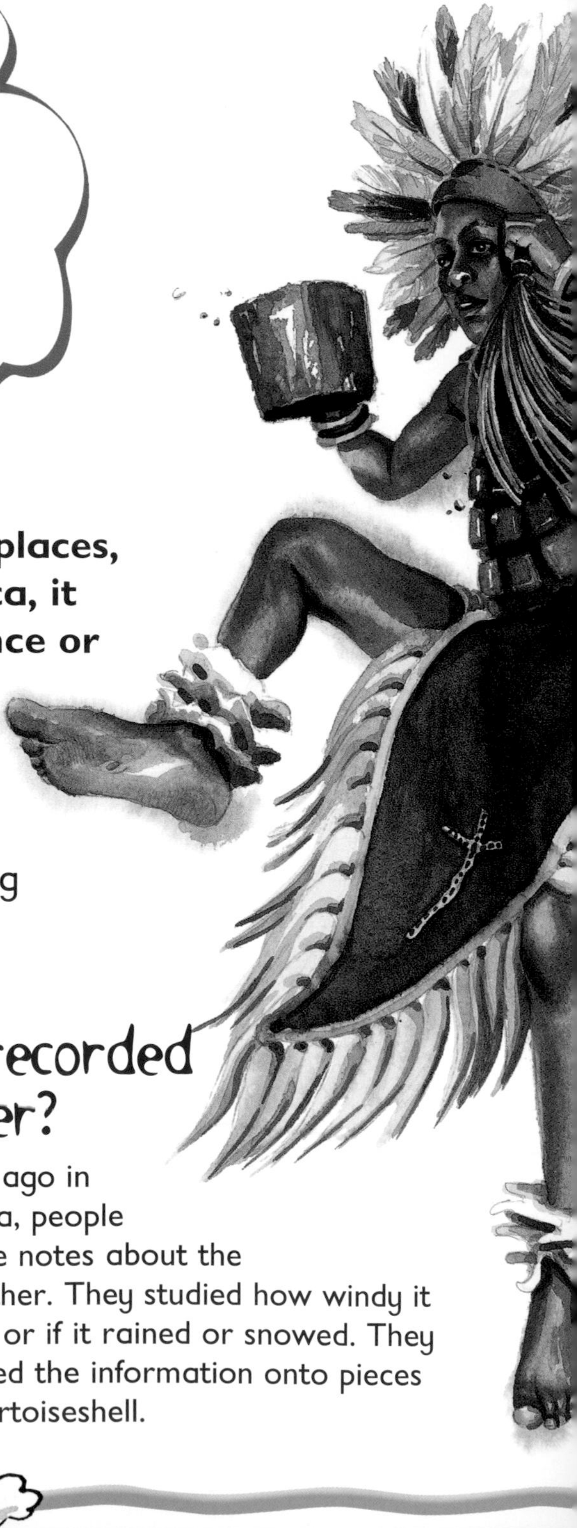

Who first recorded the weather?

Over 3000 years ago in China, people made notes about the weather. They studied how windy it was, or if it rained or snowed. They carved the information onto pieces of tortoiseshell.

Are weather sayings true?

There are many sayings about the weather. Most of them are true. One saying is 'Clear Moon, frost soon'. If there are no clouds in the sky you can see the Moon clearly. It also means it will get cold quickly at night. So the saying is true.

Rain dance

Full Moon

Weather cows!

Some people think that cows lie down when it is going to rain. But this weather saying is not true. Cows lie down on sunny days, too!

Discover

Can you find some more sayings about the weather? You could ask your teacher, or try looking in a book.

Which bird spins in the wind?

A metal cockerel on a weather vane. The cockerel spins so it can point in any direction. When the wind blows, the cockerel spins and points to where the wind is coming from. If the wind is blowing from the north, it is called a north wind. The wind blows from the north, south, east and west.

Weather vane

Groundhog Day!

In the USA, legend says that if a groundhog emerges from its burrow on 2 February and sees its shadow, winter will last for six more weeks!

What is a weather house?

A weather house is a model that can tell how much moisture is in the air. If it is going to be dry, a lady in summer clothes comes out. If it is going to be rainy, a man with an umbrella comes out.

Weather house

How do we know how hot it is?

By reading a thermometer. A thermometer shows the temperature, which is how hot the air around us is. The first thermometer was made in 1714 by Gabriel Daniel Fahrenheit.

Think

From which direction does a southerly wind blow? North or south?

Can planes tell the weather?

Weather planes don't carry any passengers. Instead they fly through the air recording the weather. They measure the temperature of the air, the speed of the wind and how much water is in the air. This information helps weather forecasters tell us what the weather is going to be like.

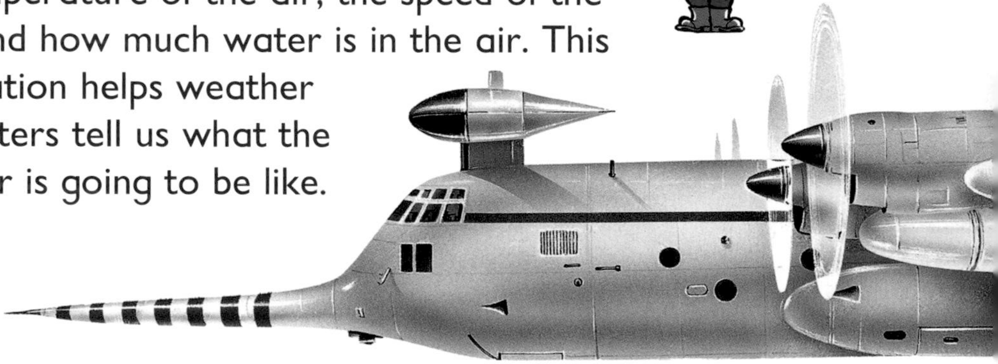

Weather plane

Astronaut snaps!

Astronauts who travel on the space shuttle and live on space stations take cameras with them. They often take amazing photographs of clouds and thunderstorms from space.

Why do scientists fly balloons?

Scientists fly balloons to find out about the weather. The balloons are filled with a gas called helium. They float up through the air and carry instruments that measure the weather. The information is sent back to the ground by radio.

How do we watch weather from space?

With weather satellites. A satellite moves around the Earth in space. It takes photographs of the clouds below and sends them back to Earth. Satellite photographs show which way hurricanes are moving. They help forecasters to warn people if a hurricane is heading their way.

Remember

Can you remember how information gets from a weather balloon down to the ground?

Did weather kill the dinosaurs?

Dinosaurs lived millions of years ago. Scientists think that they may have died because the weather all over the world got colder. They think this happened when a giant rock (meteorite) from space hit the Earth. This threw lots of dust into the air, which blocked out the Sun.

Can trees affect the weather?

Yes, they can. Many rainforests are being cut down for farming. When trees are burned, the fires release a gas called carbon dioxide. This gas acts as a blanket over the Earth and does not let heat escape. High levels of carbon dioxide can raise the temperature too much causing damage to the Earth.

Rainforest

Windy tower!

The Tower of Winds is a tower in Athens, Greece. It was built 2000 years ago. It had a giant wind vane on top to measure the direction of the wind.

Find

Can you find Greenland on a map of the world?

Is our weather changing?

Weather experts think the weather is getting warmer. If the average world temperature rises by as little 1.5°C it will mean more storms, including hurricanes and tornadoes, and more droughts too.

Quiz time

Do you remember what you have read about weather?

These questions will test your memory. The pictures will help you. If you get stuck, read the pages again.

1. Why do leaves fall in autumn?

page 39

2. When is a lake not a lake?

page 41

3. Where does it rain every day?

page 42

4. How deep is the atmosphere?

page 43

5. Are all clouds small and fluffy?

page 45

6. What rain never lands?

page 45

7. What happens in a flood?

page 46

11. What makes the sky clap?

page 52

8. Did Noah build an ark?

page 47

12. Who first recorded the weather?

page 56

9. When is snow dangerous?

page 49

13. What is a rain dance?

page 56

10. Which storm has an eye?

page 51

Answers

1. Because it is hard for them to grow in the dark winter months
2. When it's a mirage
3. In a tropical rainforest
4. Hundreds of kilometres
5. No, they come in different shapes and sizes
6. Drops that fall into very dry air
7. A lot of rain falls and floods the land
8. We don't know if Noah's ark existed
9. In an avalanche
10. A hurricane
11. A thunderstorm
12. The Chinese
13. A traditional dance to bring on clouds and rain

Questions about...

Inventions

What were the first inventions?

The first inventions were stone tools, which early people began to make about two million years ago.

During the Stone Age, about 30,000 years ago, people discovered how to sew animal skins together to make clothes. They also learnt how to keep warm and dry by building shelters.

Stone Age people using tools

How did early people see in the dark?

Prehistoric people used lamps to light up caves. The lamps were made of clay or stone saucers, which were filled with animal fat. The animal fat was then burnt using a wick made of moss.

Fire-makers!

Early people discovered how to make fire more than 250,000 years ago! Thousands of years later, flint stones were used to make sparks, which lit dried grass and wood.

Who invented the wheel?

The Sumerian people invented wheels 5500 years ago. They were heavy and made with carved wood that was fastened together. Later, the ancient Egyptians made spoked wheels, which were lighter.

Spoked wheels

Count

In this book, how many inventions can you find that use the wheel?

Who invented the first car?

Karl Benz invented the first car in 1896. It had a petrol-powered engine but could not travel very fast. The first popular car was the Model T, built in 1908 by the Ford company in the United States. Over 15 million of them were sold worldwide.

Model T Ford

Why do tractors have such big tyres?

Tractors were invented in 1892 and are used to pull farm machinery, such as ploughs. Tractors have huge tyres to stop them getting stuck in mud. Big weights at the front stop tractors tipping over when pulling heavy machinery.

Tractor

Wooden lines!

Railway tracks were once made of wood! Wheels move more easily along rails, so horses pulled wagons on wooden rails more than 400 years ago. Metal rails were invented in 1789.

What was a boneshaker?

A boneshaker was one of the first bicycles. It had solid tyres and was so uncomfortable to ride that it made people's bones shake. In 1888, John Dunlop invented air-filled rubber tyres that made cycling more comfortable.

Try

If you have a bike, try riding it in the garden. Is it a smooth or bumpy ride?

Who used the first sails?

Sails were invented by the Egyptians more than 5000 years ago. About 2000 years ago, the best sailors were the Phoenician people. They sailed in boats made of cedar wood and reeds. These ships had sails and oars and were used to make long journeys.

Draw

Using coloured pens or pencils, draw your own super sail boat. Try adding your own amazing inventions.

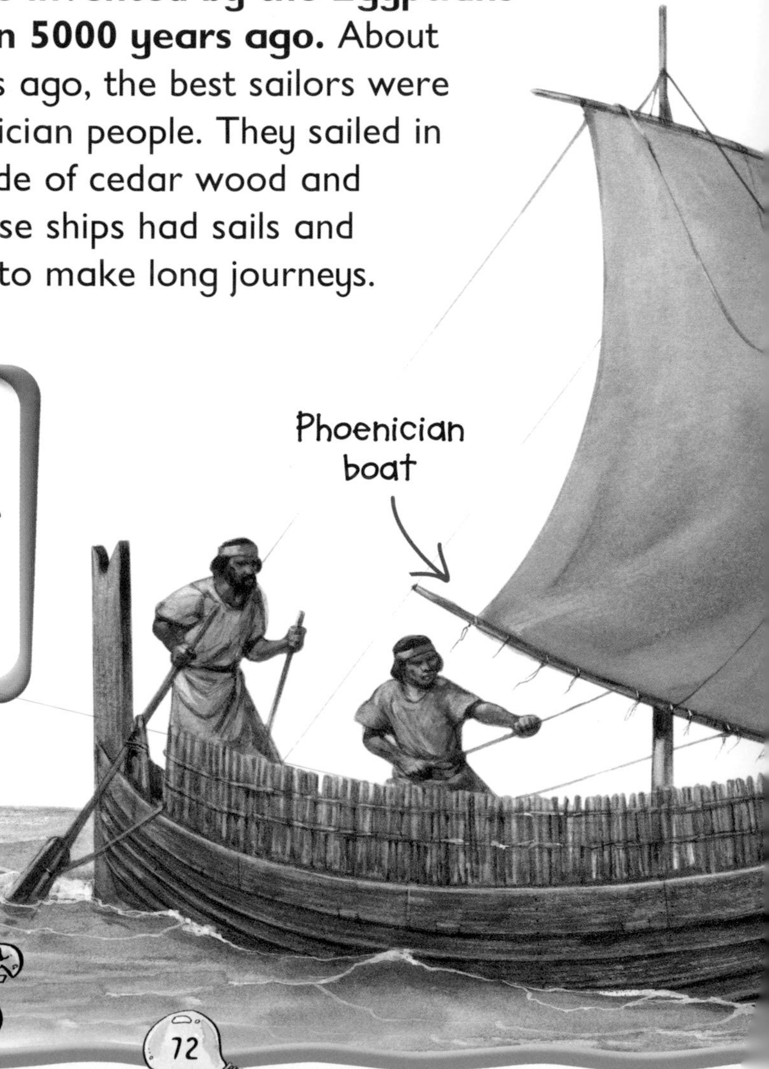

Super sailing!

Modern boats use inventions such as machines that roll up the sails and special gears that let the boat steer itself.

Why did coal miners need steam power?

Before steam power, miners had to pull coal carts out of mines by hand. This was very hard work. Then in 1814, a coal miner named George Stephenson invented an engine that pulled the carts out of the mines using steam power.

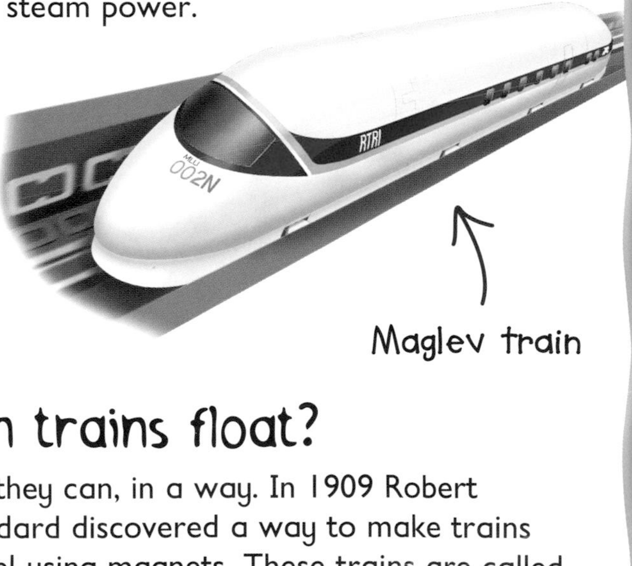

Maglev train

Can trains float?

Yes they can, in a way. In 1909 Robert Goddard discovered a way to make trains travel using magnets. These trains are called Maglevs. They run on a magnetic rail that pushes the train up so it seems to be floating. Maglevs can reach very high speeds.

What is a combine harvester?

A combine harvester is a big farm machine that cuts crops and separates grain. The first combine harvester was invented in 1836 and was pulled by horses. Today, farmers all over the world use these machines so they can harvest their crops quickly.

Plant power!

Scientists are changing the way plants grow. They have invented ways of creating crops with built-in protection from pests and diseases.

Airship

Can ships fly?

Airships can! They are filled with a special gas called helium. This gas is lighter than air, and makes the airship float in the sky. Today, airships are used to display adverts in the sky and are not used for people to travel in.

Did people pull ploughs?

Ploughs were invented in Egypt around 2000 BC and were first pulled by people. They helped farmers break up the ground and turn the soil over. Later, people began to use horses and oxen to pull ploughs.

Think

Can you think of any other machines or animals that you would find on a farm?

Who invented jumbo jets?

A jumbo jet is a plane. In 1970, the first jumbo jet flight took place between New York and London. The planes are powered by jet engines that were invented by Dr Hans von Ohain of Germany, and Sir Frank Whittle of England. Their inventions developed to become modern jet engines.

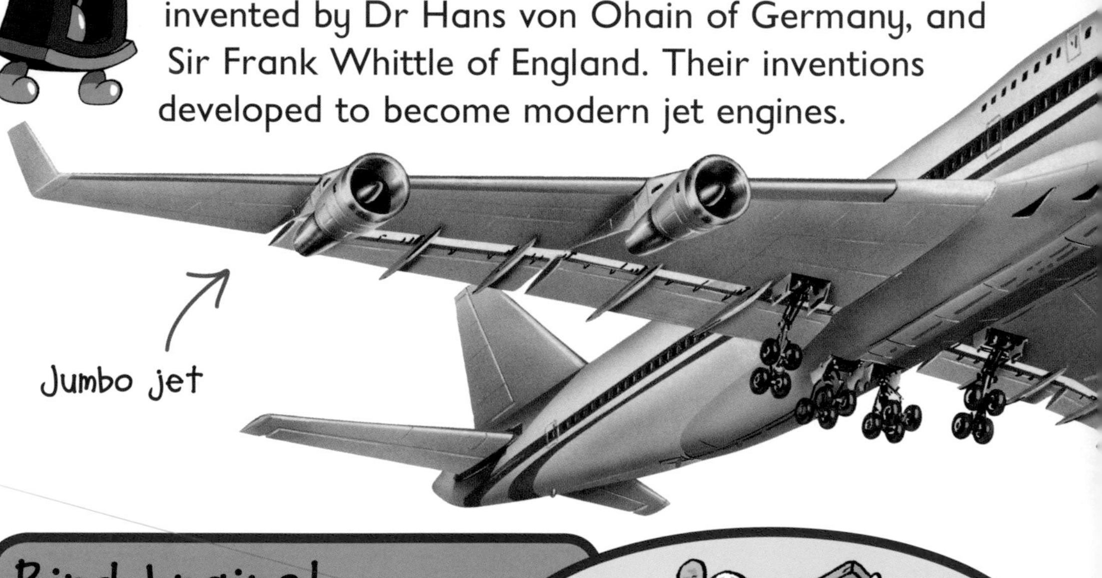

Jumbo jet

Bird brains!

Many inventors have tried to fly by flapping birdlike wings. All have failed. One of the first bird-men crashed to his death at a Roman festival in the 1st century AD.

Can balloons carry people?

Hot-air balloons were invented in 1783. They can carry people high up into the sky. The first ever passengers to fly in a hot air balloon were not humans but a cockerel, a duck and a sheep!

Do planes perform tricks?

Yes, they do. The Red Arrows are a team of highly skilled pilots that can make their planes perform tricks. Their red aircrafts can fly upside down and on their sides and are very fast. The Red Arrows perform in front of large crowds at airshows and other special occasions.

Make

With some paper, make a plane and colour it in. How far can you get it to fly?

The Red Arrows

How can we see into space?

People can look at the stars and planets by using a telescope. The first telescope was invented by a Dutchman called Hans Lippershey in 1608. In 1609, the Italian scientist Galileo built his own telescope. He was the first person to see the craters on the Moon.

Who invented spectacles?

The Italians did. In the 14th century in Italy people made their own glass lenses to look through. These small lenses were put into frames and were used to help people to read.

Write

Imagine you have found a pair of magic spectacles. Write a story about what you see when you put them on.

Microscope

How can we make small things bigger?

By using a microscope. A microscope uses pieces of glass called lenses. These make small things look bigger than they really are. The first microscope was invented in the 1600s and had one lens. Later microscopes had two lenses to make them more powerful.

Marvellous maths!

Around AD 300, the Chinese invented a counting machine called an abacus. It was a wooden frame with beads strung on wires and it helped people do complicated sums.

Who made the streets light up?

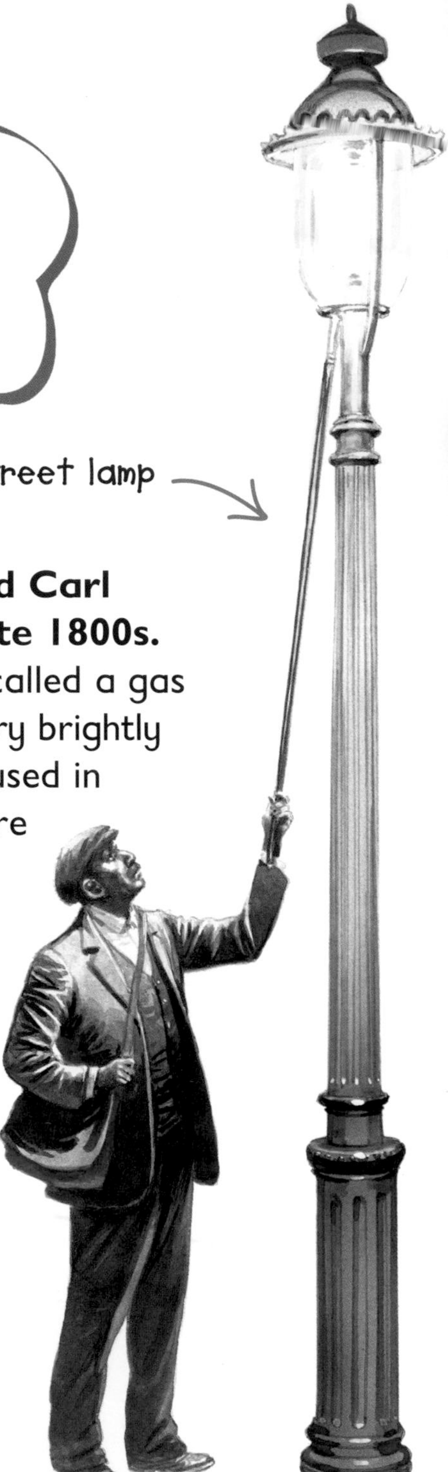

An Austrian named Carl Auer did, in the late 1800s. He invented a lamp called a gas mantle that glowed very brightly when heated up. The gas mantle was used in the first street lamps. Long torches were needed to light the lamps.

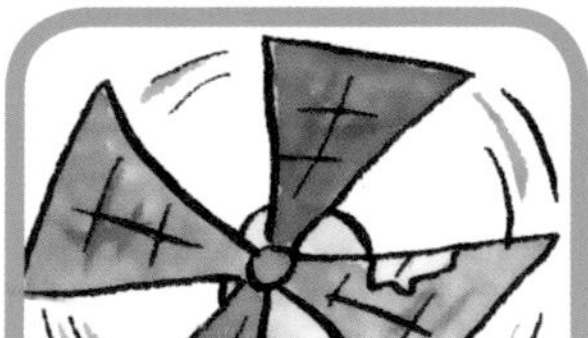

Wind power!

The first windmills were invented thousands of years ago. They helped to grind grain into flour. Today, windmills are used to pump water, make electricity and power machinery.

How big was the first computer?

The first computer was so big that it took up a whole room. In 1975, the first home computers were made but they were expensive and not very powerful. Computers today are small, cheap and powerful.

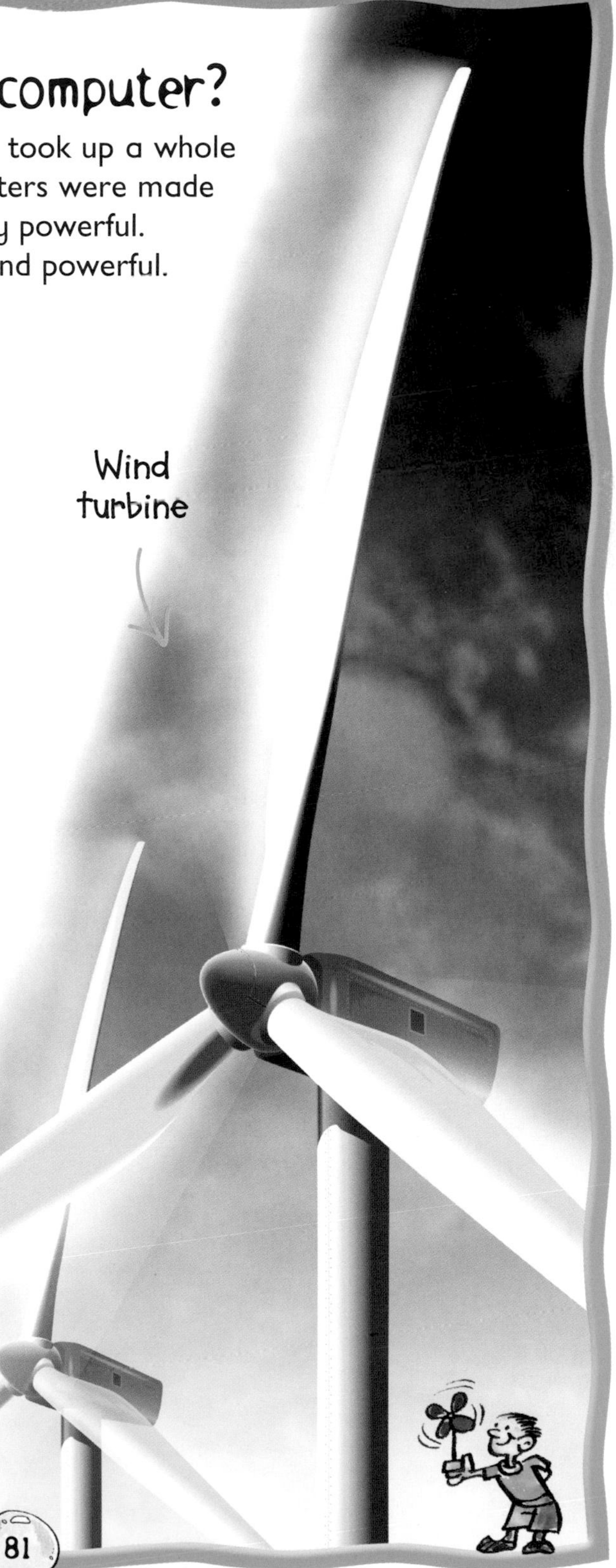

Who made electricity from the wind?

In 1888, Charles F Brush invented a modern-day windmill called a wind turbine. Wind turbines have blades that turn in the wind. These power a motor inside the turbine, which makes electricity. Wind turbines can power entire towns.

Remember

In ancient times, what was the name of the counting machine that was invented by the Chinese?

Why do clocks have hands?

Clocks have hands so that people can tell the time. The hands point to different numbers on the clock face and these tell us what time it is. Clocks work by using a series of springs and wheels that move the hands of the clock around. The first mechanical alarm clock was invented in 1787.

Make

Use a paper plate to make a clock. Write the numbers on the face and use plastic straws for the hands.

Alarm clock

How does the Sun tell the time?

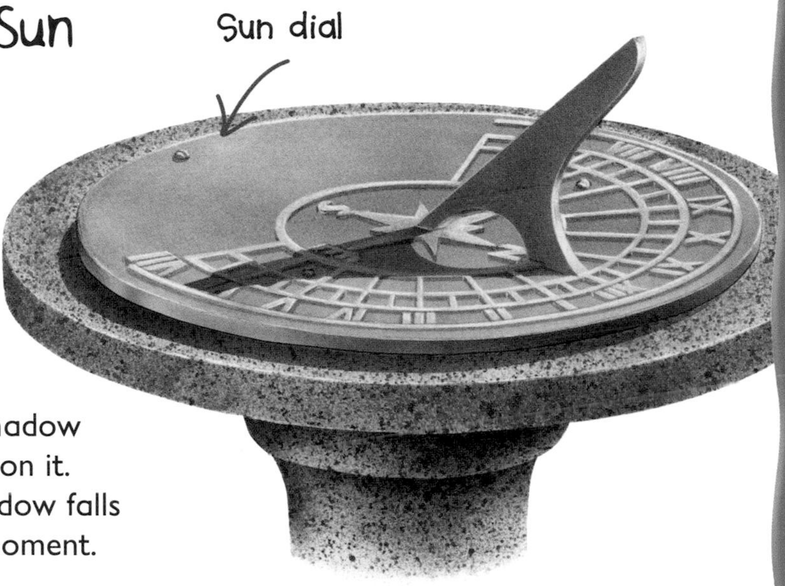

The Sun was used to help people tell the time before clocks were invented. Sundials have a stone face marked with the hours, and a pointer that makes a shadow when the Sun is shining on it. Whatever hour the shadow falls on is the time at that moment.

Watch it!

The wrist watch was invented in the 1600s by a French mathematician. He attached a piece of string to his pocket watch and tied it around his wrist.

Can candles tell the time?

Candles were once used as clocks to tell the time. They were marked with rings so that when the wax burnt down, people could tell how much time has passed by.

When was cooking invented?

Cooking was invented in prehistoric times by some of our earliest relatives. When people discovered fire, they realized that if food was placed in the fire, it tasted better. Cooking also made food safer because it killed germs that might cause sickness.

The first cooks

Write

Using pictures instead of words, write a secret message. Can your friends work out what it says?

Who wrote the first words?

The Sumerian people wrote the first words more than 5500 years ago. They scratched words onto clay tablets. The first writing was made up of pictures. Ancient picture-writing used hundreds of different signs. Today, modern alphabets have far fewer letters.

Smoky signals!

Before inventions such as the telephone, sending long-distance messages had to be simple. Native Americans used smoke signals to send messages to each other.

Who made the first phone call?

Alexander Graham Bell made the first telephone call in 1876. The telephone worked by turning vibrations in the human voice into electrical signals. These signals travelled down a wire to another phone, where they were turned back into sound.

What was a gramophone?

In 1887, Emile Berlin invented a machine that could play music. The machine was called a gramophone. To make it work, a handle was turned, which turned a disc under a steel needle. The needle allowed the music to play.

Think

Can you think of any machines in your house that you use to listen to music?

Marvellous movies!

Only one person at a time could watch the very first films. The viewer went into a special room and looked through a hole in a box.

Who invented television?

John Logie Baird invented the first television in 1926. The pictures were black and white and very blurry. Modern televisions show clear, sharp pictures in colour.

Flat screen television

Who took the first photo?

Joseph Nicephore took the first-ever photograph in 1826. The picture was of rooftops and took eight hours to take. The first cameras were very big, and instead of paper, the photos were printed on glass plates.

Why were fridges dangerous?

The first electric refrigerators were invented in 1805, but they were dangerous to use. This was because they used a poisonous gas to keep them cold. In 1929, a safer gas called freon was used. However freon causes damage to the planet, so modern fridges use a chemical called isobutane which occurs naturally.

Stone cold!

Stone Age people invented the first refrigerators! They buried any spare food in pits dug in ground that was always frozen.

Early fridge

Microwave oven

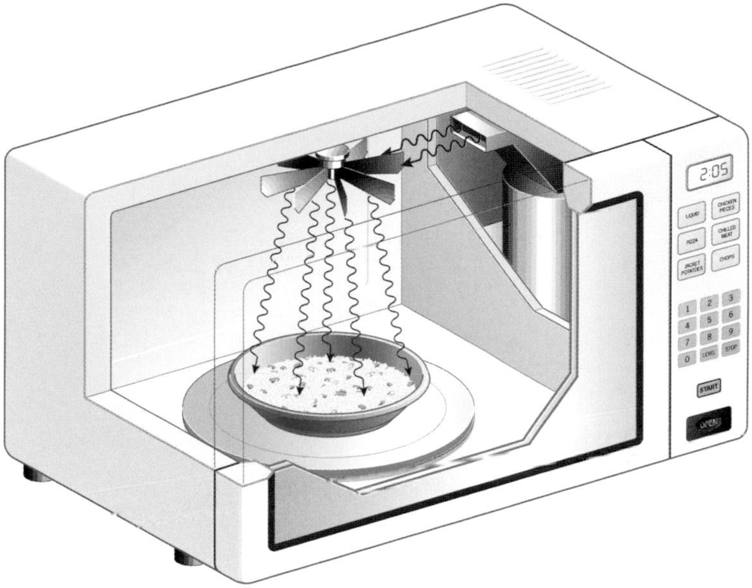

How do microwaves cook food?

A microwave oven produces waves that make food heat itself up. In 1945, Percy L. Spencer invented the microwave oven after noticing that a microwave machine at his workplace had melted a chocolate bar in his pocket.

Look

Take a look around your house. How many inventions help you and your family every day?

Have toilets always flushed?

4000 years ago in Greece, royal palaces had flushing toilets that used rainwater. Thomas Twyford invented the first ceramic flushing toilet in 1885. His design is still used today.

What was special about shuttles?

Space shuttles were very special spacecraft. This is because they were reusable. Most spacecraft can only go into space once, but the shuttle was like a space plane. It could return into space up to ten times. The first space shuttle was launched in 1981 and they were used until 2011.

Space shuttle

Write

Imagine you are living on board a space station. Write a letter to tell people about your adventure.

Who invented fireworks?

The Chinese invented fireworks thousands of years ago. The loud sound that they made was supposed to frighten off evil spirits. Today, fireworks are used to celebrate special occasions.

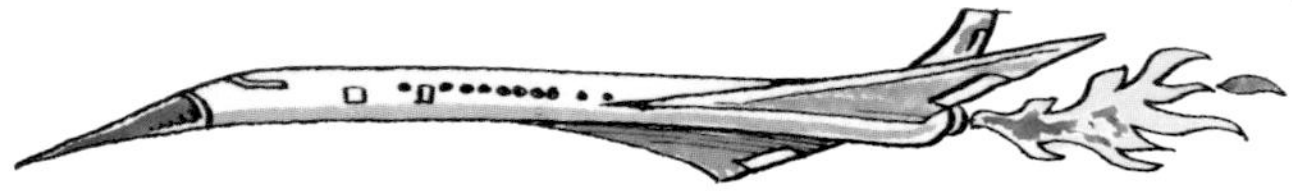

Fast flyer!

Concorde was a superfast plane that flew people across the Atlantic in record time. Trips from London to New York only took three hours.

Space station

Can people live in space?

Yes, they can. A space station is a home in space for astronauts. It has a kitchen for making meals, and cabins with sleeping bags. The first space station was launched in 1971.

Do zips have teeth?

Yes, zips do have teeth! A zip has two rows of teeth that can be opened and shut by a slider. The first zip was invented in 1891. It was called the Talon Slide Fastener and was used on a boot called the zipper. This is where the zip got its name from.

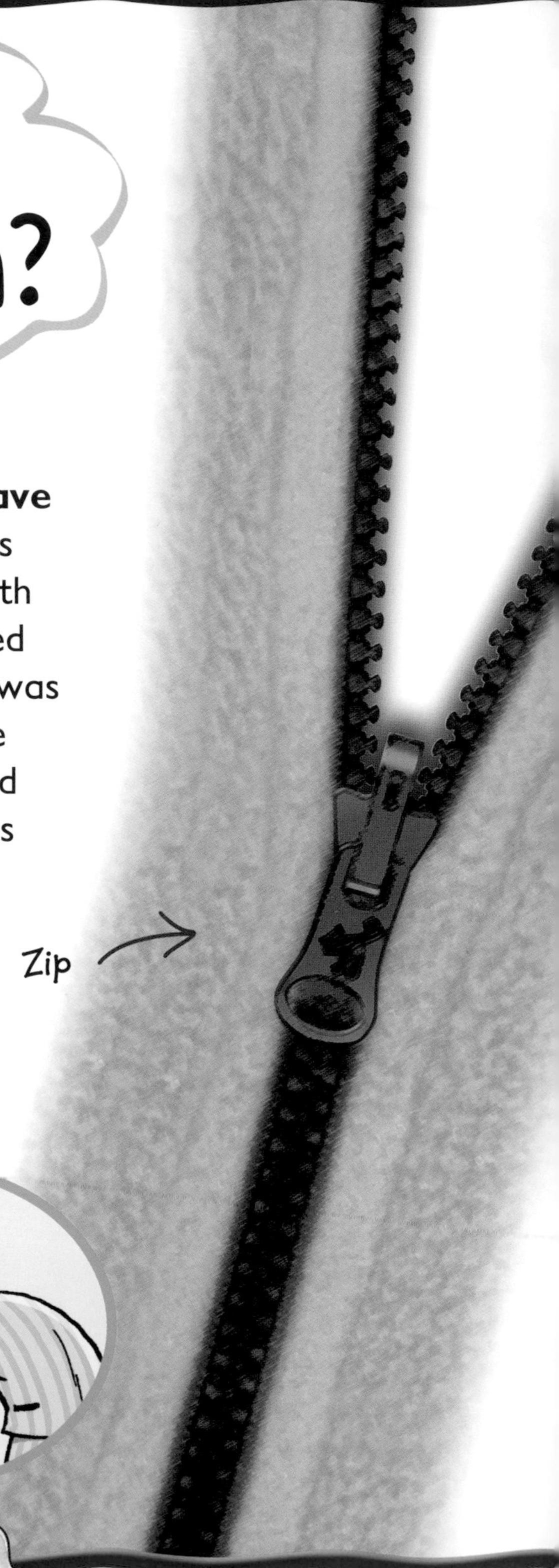

Bone brush!

The first toothbrush was made out of animal bone. The bone had small holes drilled into it where bristles were placed.

How did teddy bears get their name?

The teddy bear was named after US President Theodore Roosevelt in 1903. The president's nickname was Teddy, and once when he was out hunting he spared the life of a bear. The story spread and toy bears soon became known as teddy bears.

Which horse can rock?

The rocking horse was invented in 1780. It was a toy horse that children could ride on without hurting themselves. Early rocking horses were usually dapple-grey in colour and rocked on wooden bow rockers.

Draw

Design your own perfect toy. Draw a picture of it and colour it in.

Rocking horse

Quiz time

Do you remember what you have read about inventions? These questions will test your memory. The pictures will help you. If you get stuck, read the pages again.

page 68

1. How did early people see in the dark?

page 69

2. Who invented the wheel?

3. What was a boneshaker?

page 71

4. Can trains float?

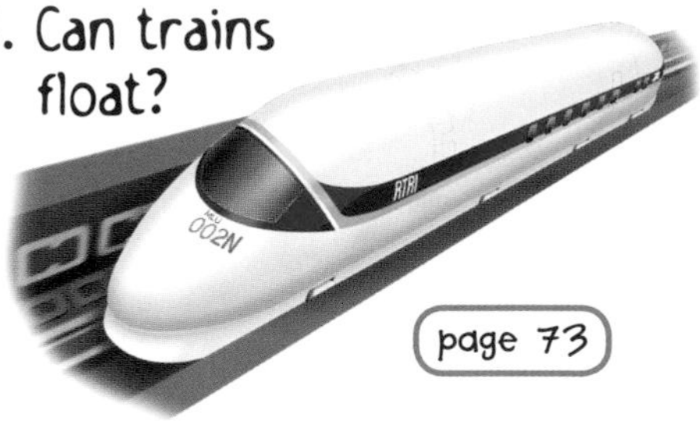

page 73

5. Did people pull ploughs?

page 75

6. Can ships fly?

page 75

7. Who invented jumbo jets?

page 76

8. Who invented spectacles?

page 79

9. How does the Sun tell the time?

page 83

10. Who wrote the first words?

page 85

page 87

11. Who took the first photo?

page 90

12. What was special about the shuttle?

page 91

13. Who invented fireworks?

Answers

1. They used lamps made of clay and animal fat
2. The Sumerian people
3. One of the very first bicycles
4. Yes, the Maglev train can
5. Yes, the first ploughs were pulled by people
6. Airships can fly
7. Dr Hans von Ohain
8. The Italians
9. With a sundial
10. The Sumerian people
11. Joseph Nicephore
12. It could be reused
13. The Chinese

Questions about...

Dinosaurs

What is a dinosaur?

Dinosaurs were animals that lived millions of years ago. There were lots of different types of dinosaur – little ones, big ones, fierce ones and shy ones. All dinosaurs lived on land – and they died out a long time ago. There are no dinosaurs living today.

Make

Use salt dough or plasticine to make some dinosaur models. Use a picture or a toy dinosaur as a guide.

When did dinosaurs live?

It is thought that the first dinosaurs lived around 252 million years ago. They roamed the Earth for the next 185 million years, before becoming extinct (dying out) about 66 million years ago. Humans haven't been around for two million years yet!

Where did the dinosaurs live?

Dinosaurs lived all over the world. At that time, the weather was much hotter than it is today. There were plants such as ferns, mosses and large evergreen trees, but there were no flowers.

What a terror!

The word 'dinosaur' means 'terrible lizard', even though dinosaurs weren't lizards! Many of the plant-eating dinosaurs were about as terrible as today's sheep!

Did any dinosaurs eat plants?

Many dinosaurs ate plants. *Plateosaurus* grew up to 8 metres long. It had a long neck and could reach high up into trees by standing on its back legs. It grabbed branches with the hooks on its thumbs and nibbled at the tastiest leaves.

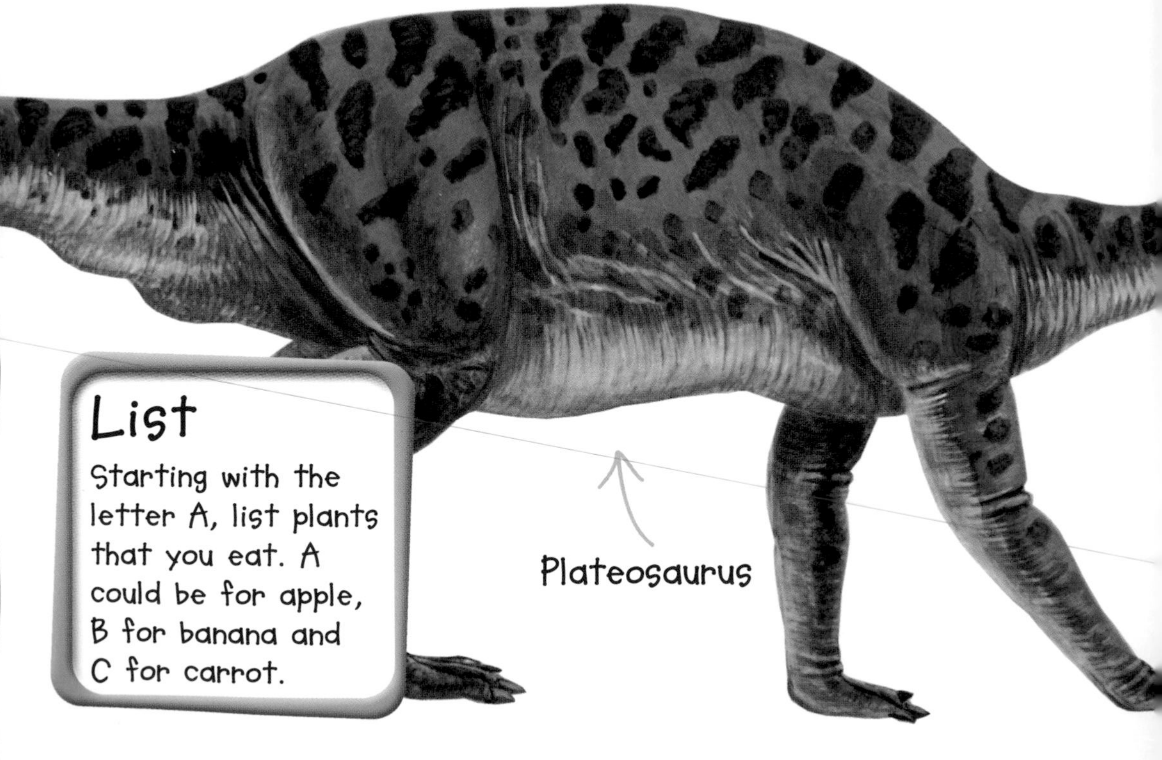

List

Starting with the letter A, list plants that you eat. A could be for apple, B for banana and C for carrot.

Why did dinosaurs eat stones?

Lots of plant-eating dinosaurs swallowed their food without chewing. Instead, they gobbled stones and pebbles, which stayed in their stomachs. When they swallowed food, the stones helped to mash the food up, turning it into a pulp.

No fruit!

Early plant-eating dinosaurs did not eat fruit or grass – none had appeared yet! Instead, they ate plants called horsetails, ferns, cycads and conifer trees.

Why were dinosaurs scaly?

Like reptiles today, such as crocodiles and alligators, dinosaurs were covered in super-tough scaly skin. The scales would have protected a dinosaur against the teeth and claws of enemies and the bites of pests such as mosquitoes and flies.

Tyrannosaurus rex

How big is a dinosaur tooth?

Dinosaur teeth were different sizes. Meat eaters, such as *Tyrannosaurus rex*, needed large, sharp and pointed teeth for tearing flesh. Each tooth measured up to 15 centimetres! When scientists look at dinosaur teeth they can work out what type of food the dinosaur ate.

Toothy!

Baryonyx had small, pointed, cone-shaped teeth. These are like the teeth of a crocodile or dolphin today. They were good for grabbing slippery food such as fish.

Did plant eaters need sharp teeth?

Plant-eating dinosaurs, such as *Apatosaurus*, had long, thin teeth that were blunt, not sharp. They used these teeth to pull leaves off branches. Herds of these dinosaurs could strip all the plants clean in one area, before moving on.

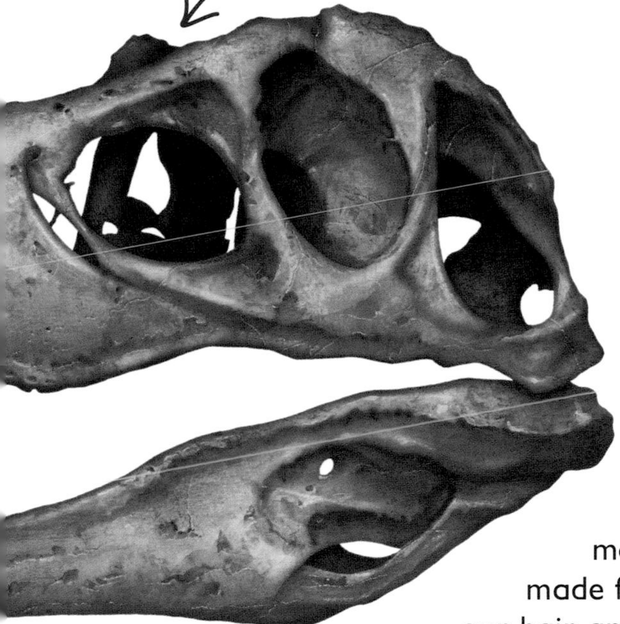

Think

You have different types of teeth. Think about which ones you use to cut food, and which ones you use to chew.

Did all dinosaurs have teeth?

Not all dinosaurs needed teeth. *Ornithomimus* had a beak-shaped mouth without teeth. Its mouth was made from the same tough substance as our hair and nails. This bird-like dinosaur probably pecked at seeds, worms and bugs. Its large eyes helped it to find food.

What were the biggest dinos?

The biggest dinosaurs, called sauropods, were ENORMOUS! Each one could weigh as much as ten elephants. *Brachiosaurus* was one of the largest dinosaurs that ever lived and was 25 metres long. It was twice as tall as a giraffe and could reach the tops of the tallest trees.

Draw

Lots of animals eat plants and live in groups, or herds. Draw some modern animals that spend all day eating plants.

How big were the biggest dinosaurs that ever lived?

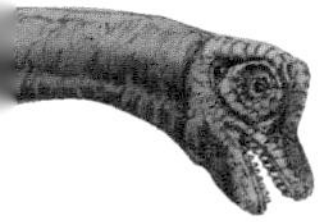

One of the biggest dinosaurs ever discovered is *Argentinosaurus*. Not much is known about this giant, but it is thought that it may have measured 40 metres from head to tail! *Argentinosaurus* had a huge body but a small head and brain.

Scary tail!

Diplodocus is also known as 'Old Whip-tail'! It could swish its tail so hard that it made a CRACK! like a whip. This would scare off enemies or even rip off their skin.

What did sauropods eat?

All sauropods ate plants. They probably had to spend most of the day eating, just to get enough energy for their enormous, heavy bodies. They may have spent 20 hours every day just grazing and nibbling at plants.

Why did dinosaurs have claws?

Most dinosaurs had claws on their fingers and toes. Meat-eating dinosaurs, such as *Deinonychus* (die-non-ee-kus) used their claws for catching and killing other animals. These dinosaurs were fast, clever and strong. Their claws could cut like knives and their teeth were razor-sharp.

Discover

Look at books to find pictures of elephants' feet. Do their toenails look like the claws of Apatosaurus?

Were all claws sharp?

Even plant-eating dinosaurs, such as sauropods, had claws. They didn't need claws to catch other animals, so they were flat and blunt rather than sharp. *Apatosaurus* had claws to protect its feet from stones, just like nails protect your fingertips and toes.

Thumb nose!

When scientists discovered remains of *Iguanodon*, they found a bone shaped like a horn. They put this on *Iguanadon's* nose. Now they think it is a thumb claw!

Which dinosaur had a spike on each hand?

Iguanodon was a plant-eating dinosaur. It didn't need spikes to kill other animals, but it could use them as weapons to defend itself.

If meat-eating dinosaurs attacked *Iguanodon*, it could fight back with its strong arms, using its spikes like daggers.

What was the scariest dinosaur?

***Tyrannosaurus rex* – known as *T-rex* for short – is one of the scariest dinosaurs.** This dinosaur was a large meat eater. It had powerful legs that helped it run fast and a huge mouth filled with lots of sharp, pointed teeth.

Colour

No one knows what colour dinosaurs were. Draw your favourite dinosaur, then colour it in using spots, stripes and colours!

Giganotosaurus

How big were the biggest meat-eating dinosaurs?

Giganotosaurus was even bigger than *T-rex* – it is one of the largest meat-eating dinosaurs ever found. Its huge legs could carry more than 8 tonnes of weight, even when it was chasing its prey. It had small arms and both had three claws for grabbing and stabbing.

How did meat eaters get their food?

Some meat eaters hunted and captured their prey using their powerful claws and sharp teeth. Others were scavengers. This means that they ate any dead animals that they found. It is thought that *T-rex* both hunted, and scavenged, for food.

Bite marks!

Some meat-eating dinosaurs not only bit their prey, but also each other! Remains of a T-rex had bite marks on its head. Perhaps the dinosaurs fought each other to become leader of the pack.

Which dinosaur had big eyes?

Dinosaurs used their senses to see, touch, hear, smell and taste. *Troodon* was a bird-like dinosaur that had HUGE eyes. Scientists think it may have hunted at night, and that its large eyes helped it to find food in the dark.

Play

Play a game of hide and seek. Use your senses, such as seeing and hearing, to hunt your prey!

What were the noisiest dinosaurs?

We can't be sure what sounds dinosaurs made, but *Parasaurolophus* was probably one of the noisiest! It had a large crest on its head that was made of hollow bone. *Parasaurolophus* could have blown air through the crest to make a bellowing noise, like a giant trumpet.

Were dinosaurs clever or stupid?

Animals with big brains are usually cleverer than those with small brains. *Apatosaurus* had a tiny brain. *Troodon* had a large brain, compared to the size of its body. It may have been one of the cleverest dinosaurs that ever lived.

Dino rap!

Small meat-eating dinosaurs are called 'raptors'. These dinos lived and hunted in packs. They were slim, clever and fast. Some even had feathers to keep them warm!

How fast could dinosaurs move?

Some dinosaurs could run very fast – up to 80 kilometres an hour. That is faster than a horse at full gallop! *Ornithomimus* could run this fast because it had a slim body, hollow bones and long, thin legs. It ran fast so it could chase other animals, and escape being eaten itself!

Print

Dip feathers in paint and press them on paper to make your own prints. Try making handprints, too.

Could big dinosaurs move quickly?

Large dinosaurs were often slower. Heavy bodies were harder to move! *Muttaburrasaurus* was a big dinosaur that may have run on its hind legs, holding its head up to look for enemies. Its long tail may have helped it to keep its balance.

Speedy!

Coelophysis (co-el-off-ee-sis) could trot, jump and leap. It ran upright on its two back legs. It could also bound along on all four legs like a dog, at speeds of 30 kilometres an hour.

Were some dinosaurs small?

All dinosaurs were quite small when they first hatched from their eggs! Some fully-grown dinosaurs were not much bigger than a pet cat. *Compsognathus* was a small, light dinosaur that ate little creatures, such as lizards and bugs.

Did dinosaurs wear armour?

Dinosaurs needed to protect themselves from their enemies. Some of them did this by growing great pieces of bone over their bodies. These bony plates protected the dinosaurs' soft bodies underneath, like huge shields, or suits of armour.

Which dinosaur had a lumpy tail?

Euoplocephalus (you-o-plo-sef-a-lus) had a tail that was strengthened with lumps of bone. When this dinosaur swung its tail, it could hit an attacker with such force that it could break a leg!

Blink!

The armoured dinosaur Euoplocephalus (you-o-plo-sef-al-us) was so well-protected that it even had bony plates on its eyelids, which could snap open and closed, just like shutters!

Which dinosaur had three horns?

Triceratops was a plant eater and it probably used its three horns to frighten away attackers. It would also have used them for fighting enemies. *Triceratops* looked scary, but it probably spent most of its time quietly eating plants.

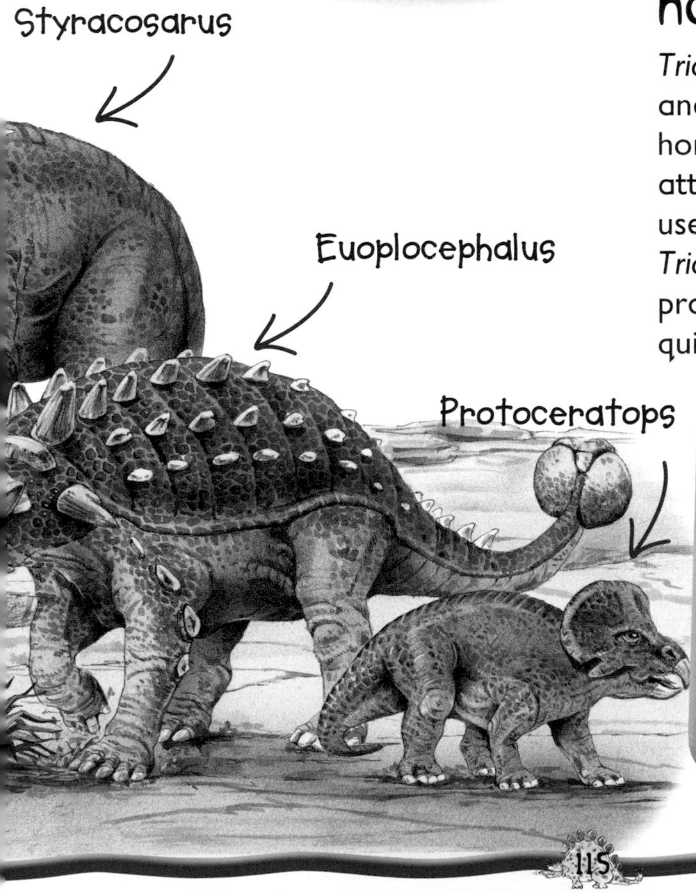

Make

Make a dinosaur model from clay or dough and then add a suit of armour. Include horns and a tail-club, using cardboard or pebbles.

How did dinosaurs have babies?

Dinosaurs laid eggs, just like birds, lizards and crocodiles do today. *Protoceratops* was a small dinosaur, the size of a pig. It lived in the desert. The female made a bowl-shaped nest in the warm sand and then laid her eggs inside it.

Find out

Find out how much you weighed and how long you were when you were born. Ask how quickly you grew!

Did dinosaurs look after their babies?

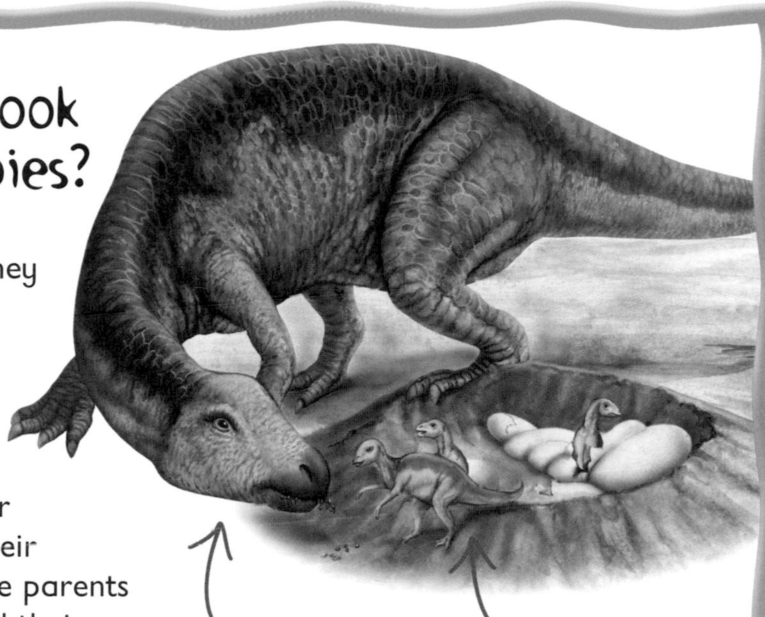

Some dinosaurs did look after their babies, until they were old enough to look after themselves. *Maiasaura* collected food for its newly hatched young and fed it to them, rather like birds feed their chicks today. The parents probably guarded their babies, too.

How do we know about dinosaur babies?

Scientists have found dinosaur eggs, and the remains of nests that have lasted for millions of years. They have even discovered large areas where many *Maiasaura* mothers came to lay their eggs, year after year.

Big baby!

Baby dinosaurs grew up to five times faster than human babies! A baby dinosaur, such as Diplodocus, was already one metre long and 30 kilograms in weight when it came out of its egg!

Did dinosaurs live alone?

Some dinosaurs lived alone, but many lived in groups, or herds. *Velociraptor* was a fast runner and meat eater that lived in packs. Just like today's lions and wolves, *Velociraptor* could kill bigger animals than itself. These dinosaurs hunted together.

Fossil poo!

Dinosaur droppings also form fossils! These have pieces of food inside such as bones or plants. Some fossil droppings are as big as TV sets!

Could dinosaurs leap and jump?

Scientists work out how dinosaurs moved by looking at their bones. The bones of *Coelophysis* are small, hollow and light so it was probably able to dart about easily. The shapes of its teeth and jaw bones suggest that *Coelophysis* ate insects or fish.

Look

Look at some pictures of birds such as ostriches. Do they remind you of any dinosaurs in this book?

Why are some dinosaurs like birds?

Some dinosaurs had feathers, large eyes and beaks. They even laid eggs and ate insects. It is believed that some changed (evolved) over time and became the very first birds on Earth.

Why did the dinosaurs die?

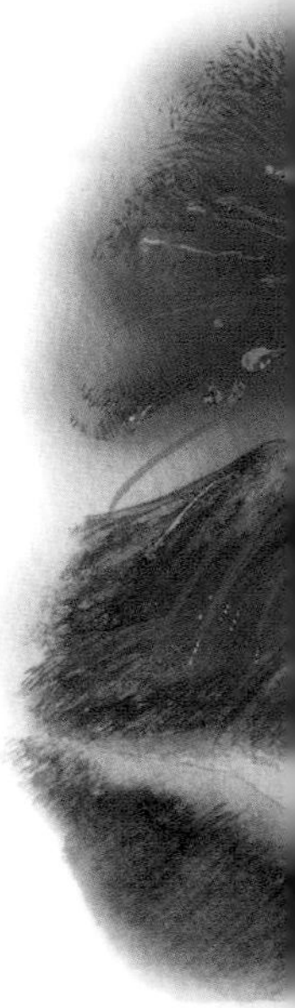

About 65 million years ago the dinosaurs suddenly died (became extinct). No one knows for sure why this happened, but something HUGE must have taken place to affect all life on the planet.

Read

Go to the library to find out about animals today that are in danger of becoming extinct. Find out why.

The dinosaurs may have been killed by a giant rock from space

Erupting volcanoes

What killed millions of animals?

Maybe volcanoes erupted, spitting out enormous clouds of ash and poisonous gas. Maybe a large lump of rock from space (a meteorite) smashed into the Earth. These things can change the weather, so perhaps the dinosaurs died because it got too cold for them.

Egg hunters!

Some dinosaurs might have become extinct because their eggs were eaten by other animals. Shrew-like creatures around at the time may have eaten the eggs at night as dinosaurs slept.

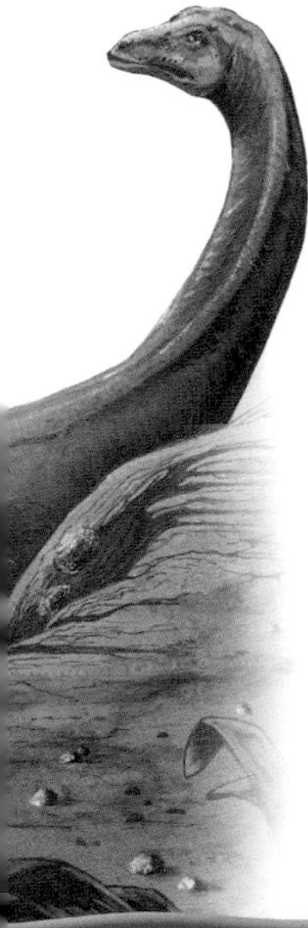

Could the dinosaurs have died from a disease?

This is unlikely because it wouldn't explain why so many millions of other animals died too. It is thought that more than two-thirds of all living things died at the same time as the dinosaurs, including sea creatures and plants.

Can we find new dinosaurs?

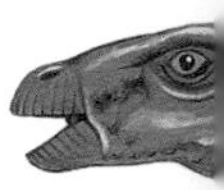

The remains of animals and plants that lived long ago are called fossils. These remains are bones, teeth, eggs and footprints – that have turned to rock over millions of years. Fossils of dinosaurs such as *Jobaria* and *Janenschia* have been found in Africa.

Think

If you found fossils from a new dinosaur, think of what name you would give your own dinosaur.

Dino girl!

Leaellynasaura (lee-ell-in-oh-saw-ra) was named after the daughter of the scientists who found its fossils!

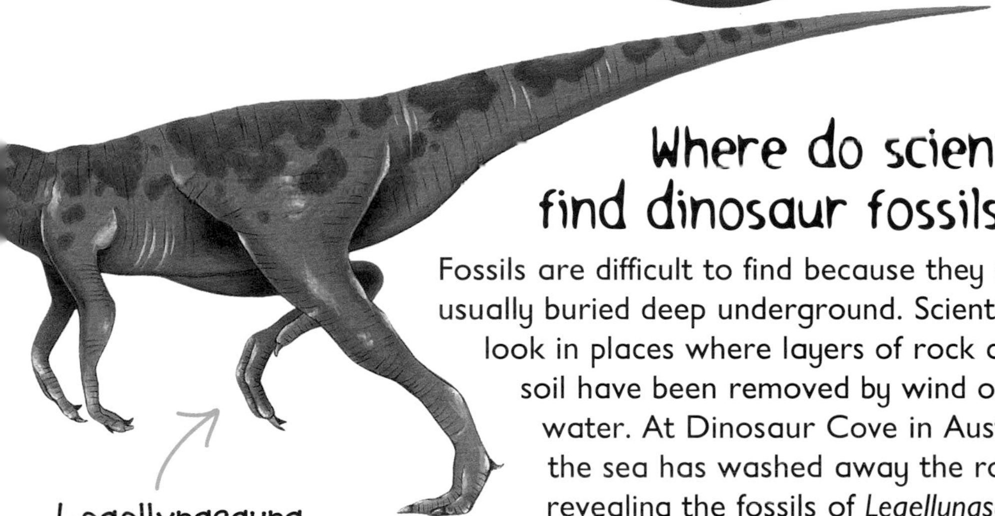

Where do scientists find dinosaur fossils?

Fossils are difficult to find because they are usually buried deep underground. Scientists look in places where layers of rock and soil have been removed by wind or water. At Dinosaur Cove in Australia the sea has washed away the rock, revealing the fossils of *Leaellynasaura*.

Could dinosaurs ever come back to life?

It is unlikely that dinosaurs will ever walk the Earth again. However, scientists are still finding fossils and using them to uncover new facts about the lives of these magnificent creatures. Dinosaurs live on, but only in our imaginations!

Quiz time

Do you remember what you have read about dinosaurs? These questions will test your memory. The pictures will help you. If you get stuck, read the pages again.

page 101

1. Why did dinosaurs eat stones?

page 102

2. How big is a dinosaur tooth?

3. What were the biggest dinos?

page 104

4. What was the scariest dinosaur?

page 108

5. How big were the biggest meat-eating dinosaurs?

page 109

6. Which dinosaur had big eyes?

page 110

7. Were some dinosaurs small?

page 113

page 120

11. Why did the dinosaurs die?

8. Which dinosaur had a lumpy tail?

page 115

12. Where do scientists find dinosaur fossils?

page 123

9. Did dinosaurs look after their babies?

page 117

13. Could dinosaurs ever come back to life?

page 123

10. Could dinosaurs leap and jump?

page 119

Answers

1. To mash food up in their stomachs
2. Different sizes
3. Sauropods
4. Tyrannosaurus rex
5. Even bigger than T-Rex
6. Troodon
7. Yes, some were not much bigger than pet cats
8. Euoplocephalus
9. Yes, some did
10. Yes, Coelophysis could
11. Volcanoes may have erupted, or a meteorite may have smashed into the Earth
12. In rocks
13. No

Questions about...

Bugs

Are all bugs insects?

Insects are the largest of all the animal groups. There are millions of different kinds that live almost everywhere in the world. Not all bugs are insects. Spiders belong to a group called arachnids, and millipedes are in yet another group called myriapods.

Garden spider is an arachnid

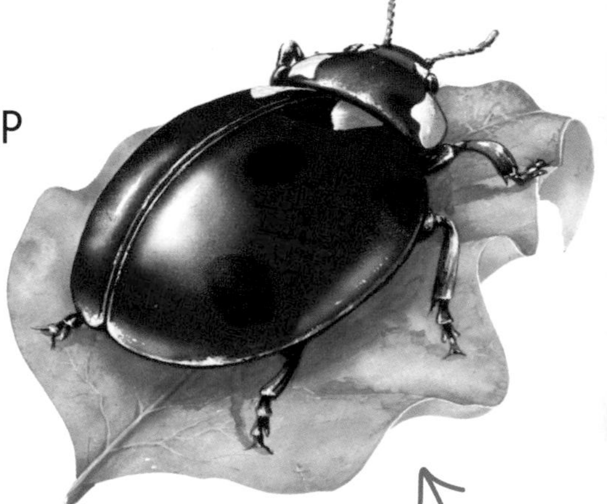

Ladybird is an insect

Pill millipede is a myriapod

Dinner date!

Breeding time is very dangerous for the praying mantis. After mating, the female may eat the male.

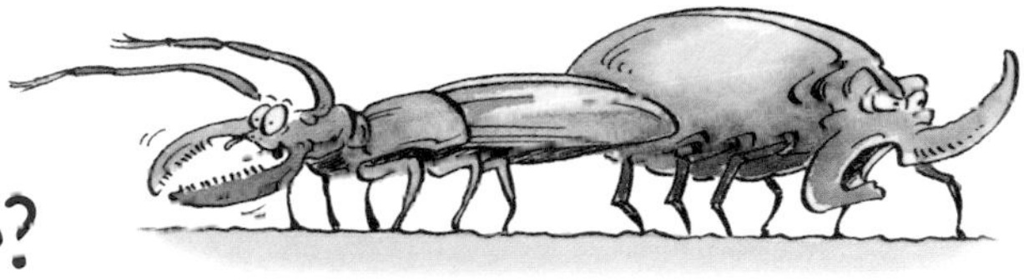

How many wings does an insect have?

Most Insects have two pairs of wings and they use them to fly from place to place. A large moth flaps its wings once or twice each second, whilst some tiny flies flap their wings almost 1000 times each second.

Moth

Do insects have skeletons?

Insects do not have a bony skeleton inside their bodies like we do. Instead, their bodies are covered by a series of horny plates. This is called an exoskeleton.

Look

Have a look in your garden, under rocks and in the soil. How many different insects can you find?

Where do butterflies come from?

① Caterpillar hatches from an egg

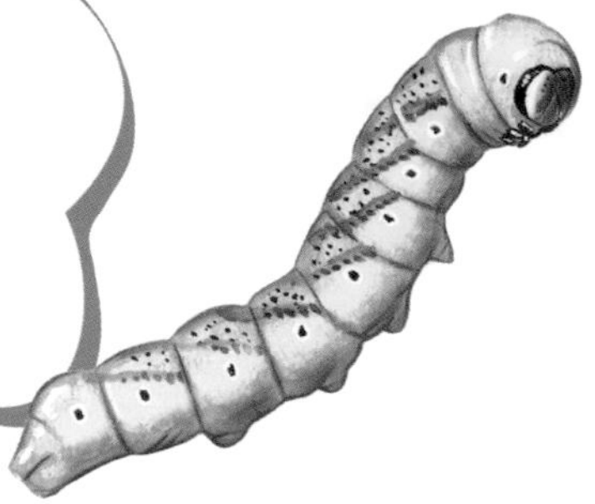

Butterflies start off life as caterpillars – wriggly grubs that hatch from eggs. Caterpillars eat lots of leaves, and when they are big enough, they attach themselves to twigs. They form hard shells called pupas. Inside the pupa, the caterpillar changes into a butterfly. When the butterfly is fully formed, it breaks out of its pupa.

② Pupa is formed

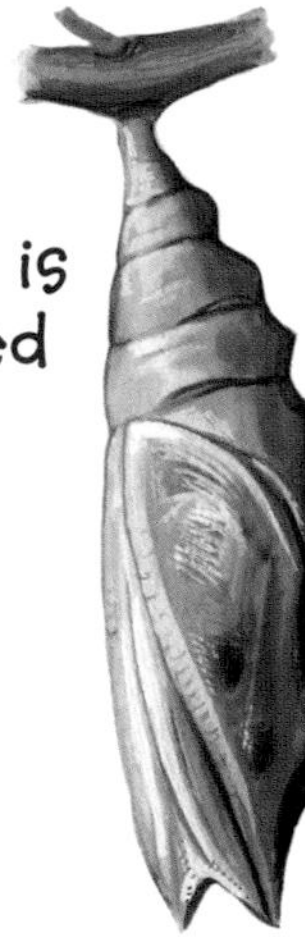

③ Butterfly breaks out of its pupa

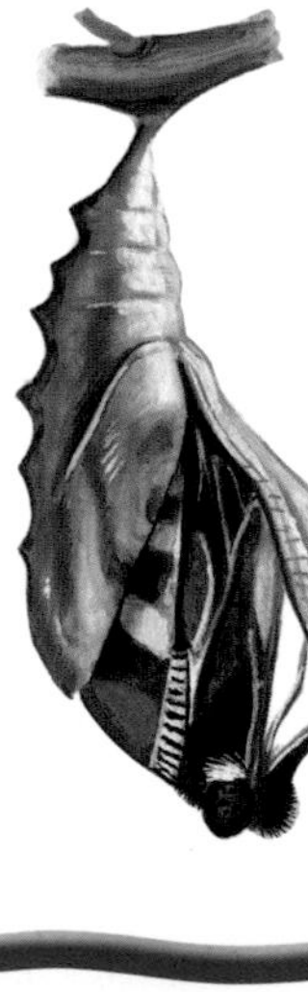

Fast mover!

The green tiger beetle is a fast-moving hunter that races over open ground. It chases smaller creatures such as ants, woodlice, worms and spiders.

④ Butterfly flies away

Peacock butterfly

Paint

Fold some paper in half. Open it up and paint two butterfly wings on one side. Fold it again and open it up to see all of the butterfly.

How far can a flea jump?

Fleas can jump a very long distance for their body size. These tiny insects measure just 2 to 3 millimetres in length. They can jump over 30 centimetres, which is more than 100 times their body size.

Flea

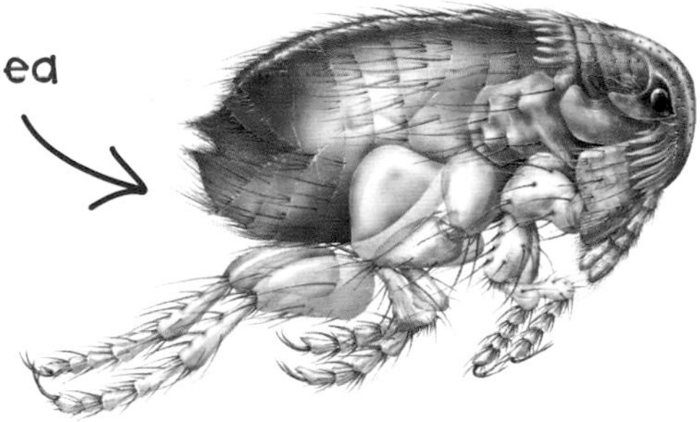

Which butterfly flies the highest?

One of the strongest insect fliers is the Apollo butterfly. It can fly high over hills and even mountains, then it rests on a rock or flower in the sunshine.

Why are butterflies brightly coloured?

Like many butterflies, the monarch butterfly has bright, bold colours on its wings. These warn other animals, such as birds and lizards, that it tastes horrible and is not good for them to eat.

Tasty treats!

Animal droppings are delicious to many kinds of insects. Various beetles lay their eggs in dung. The young insects then hatch out and eat it.

Where do cockroaches live?

Just about everywhere! Cockroaches are beetles that run quickly across the ground. They have low, flat bodies and can dart into small spaces under logs, stones and bricks. They can also hide in cupboards, furniture – and beds!

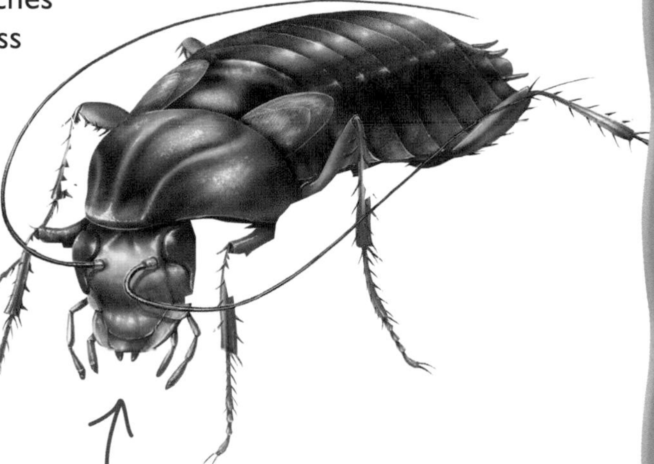

Cockroach

Monarch butterfly

Think

Write a list of any fast-running animals that you can think of.

Can insects walk on water?

Some insects can. The pondskater has a slim, light body with long, wide legs, which allow it to glide across the surface of the water.

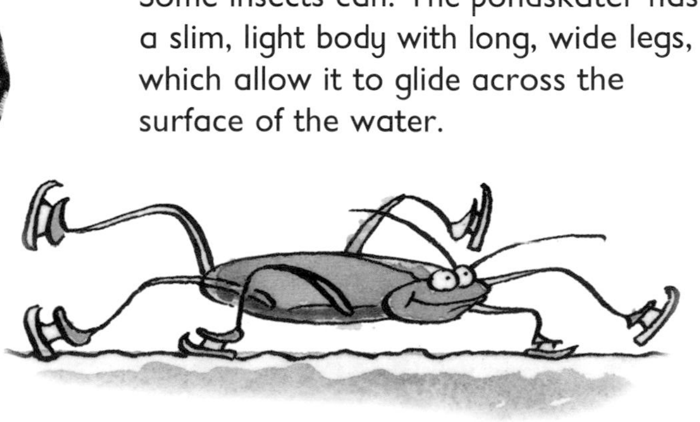

Why do bees make honey?

Bees make sweet, sticky honey packed with energy. Wild bees make honey to feed themselves and their growing young, which are called larvae. Lots of animals eat honey, including humans, who keep honeybees in nests called hives so that the honey is easier to collect.

How many times can a bee sting you?

A bee can only sting once in its whole lifetime. After a bee jabs its sting into an enemy, the sting stays in its victim. As the bee flies away, the rear part of its body tears off and the bee soon dies.

Yummy!

Ants get food from insects called aphids. When an ant strokes an aphid, it oozes a drop of 'milk' called honeydew, which the ant then drinks.

Taste

Ask an adult if you can taste some honey. See if you think it tastes sweet and sticky, too.

Why do bees have a queen?

The queen bee lays all of the eggs, from which young bees hatch. Without her, there would be no other bees. Worker bees look after the queen and the eggs.

Why do spiders make silk?

Spiders make very thin, fine threads called silk. Some spiders use their silk to make webs to catch their prey. Other spiders wrap up their victims in silk to stop them escaping. Female spiders make silk bags called cocoons and lay their eggs in them.

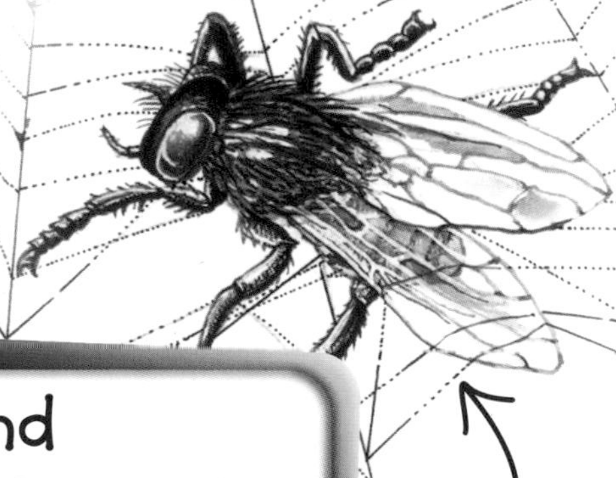

Can spiders spit?

The spitting spider can. It feeds on mosquitoes, moths and flies. When it spots its prey, it spits a sticky silk thread over it. This stops the victim moving, so the spider can eat it.

Find

See if you can find a spider's web. Look in the corners of windows, in garages and in sheds.

Do spiders have fangs?

Spiders have sharp fangs in their jaws, which they use to grab and bite their prey. The fangs inject a poison to kill the victim. The spider then eats its food by sucking out the body juices.

Crowded house!

A wasps' nest may have about 2000 wasps in it, but a termite colony may have over five million termites.

Why do crickets chirp?

Male crickets chirp to attract the attention of female crickets. Their wings have hard, ridged strips at the base like a row of pegs, which make a chirping sound when they are rubbed together.

Pretend

Make your own insect noise and pretend to be an insect. Can you chirp like a cricket?

What is a termite?

Termites are small insects that are similar to ants. They live in large groups called colonies, which include king, queen, worker and soldier termites. Soldier termites protect the rest of the colony and have large jaws that they use as weapons.

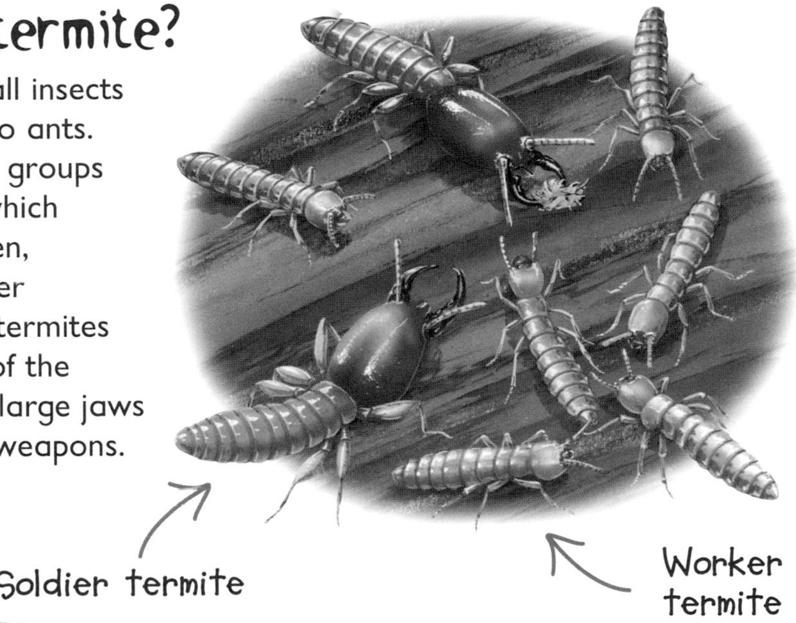

Fantastic flies!

In winter, flies die from cold and hunger. Before they die, they lay eggs in sheltered places so that next year new flies will hatch.

Which insect can eat a house?

Termites can damage wooden houses by making their nests inside the wood. The damage cannot be seen from the outside until the wood is almost hollow. If anyone touches it, the house might collapse.

Which insect is a flying hunter?

Dragonflies are fierce flying hunters. Their huge eyes spot tiny prey such as midges and mayflies. They dash through the air and use their legs to catch their victims. Then they fly back to their perch to eat their meal.

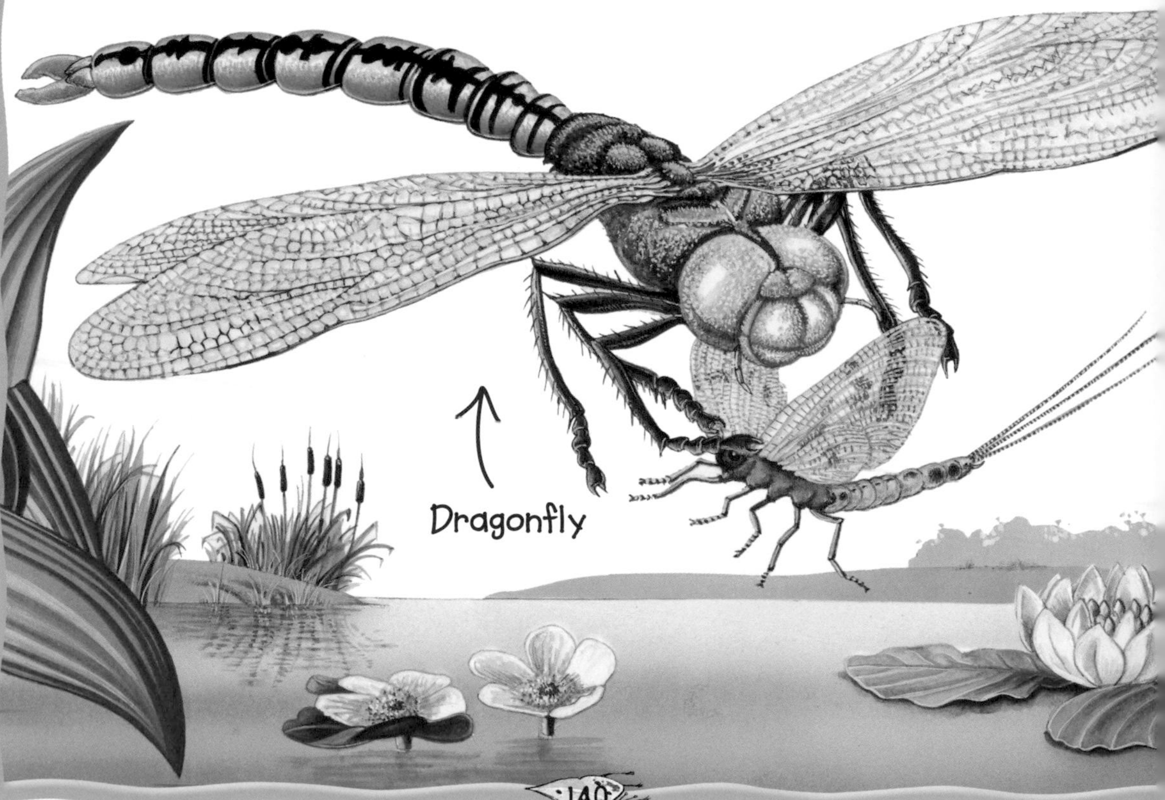

Do insects like to pray?

The praying mantis is named because its front legs are folded, as if it is praying. In fact, it is waiting to grab some food. It waits for a fly or moth to come near, then SNAP! It grabs the victim very quickly with its front legs.

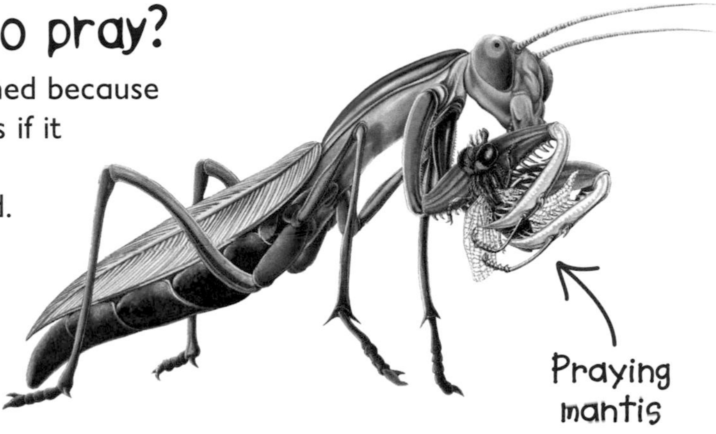

Remember

Can you remember what dragonflies like to eat? Read these pages again to find out.

Can insects spread disease?

Many insects spread germs and disease. The mosquito is one of the deadliest. In hotter parts of the world, when it bites people to suck their blood, it may pass on a terrible illness such as malaria or yellow fever.

Playing dead!

When in danger, the click beetle falls onto its back and pretends to be dead. When the danger has gone, it arches its body and then straightens out with a jerk and a 'click'!

Why are scorpions' tails so deadly?

Scorpions have poisonous stings at the end of their tails. They use them to attack their victims. Scorpions may also wave their tails at enemies to warn them that, unless they go away, they will sting them to death!

Which beetle carries a spray gun?

The bombardier beetle squirts out a spray of smelly liquid from its rear end, almost like a small spray gun! This startles and stings an attacker and gives the beetle time to escape.

Discover

Spiders and scorpions belong to the same family group. Try and find out what the group is called.

Scary spiders!

The name 'tarantula' was first given to a type of wolf spider from Europe. Tarantulas are the biggest type of spider and live in hot parts of the world.

What is the deadliest spider?

Black widow spiders are the most feared and dangerous of all spiders. They are small, shiny and black and they have a poisonous bite that can kill people. After mating, the female black widow spider may eat the male.

Black widow spider

Why are there spiders in the bath?

Hornet

House spiders don't go in the bath to get clean. They hunt at night, and may slide into a bath by accident. The sides of the bath are too steep and slippery for them to climb out.

Hornet-moth

When is a hornet not a hornet?

The hornet-moth looks similar to a large type of wasp known as a hornet. This wasp has a very painful sting, but the hornet-moth is harmless. However, few other creatures dare to eat it as they think it is a wasp.

Grow up!

The American cicada is a kind of grasshopper. Its young live underground and they can take 17 years to change into adults!

Can ants join the army?

Ants don't really join the army. Army ants, travel in large groups of about 10,000 insects. They crawl in long lines through the forest, eating whatever they can bite and overpower, including spiders, lizards and birds.

Play

With a group of friends, get in a line and march around like a group of army ants.

Why do ladybirds have spots?

Ladybirds have bright pink, yellow or red bodies that are covered in black spots. These bright colours and spots tell other animals not to eat them, as they don't taste very nice.

Which insect glows at night?

Fireflies are not flies but a type of beetle. They produce a green or yellow light from their stomachs to attract a partner. Fireflies live on plants and trees during the day and are only active at night.

Firefly

Think

Can you name any other insects or animals that have spots?

Sticking around!

Stick and leaf insects look exactly like sticks and leaves. When the wind blows, they rock and sway in the breeze like real twigs and leaves.

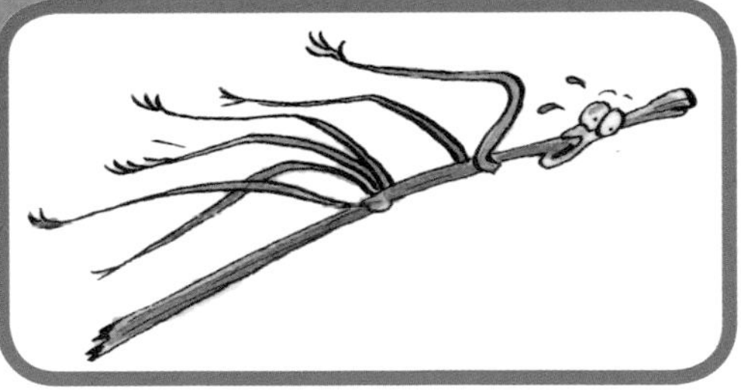

Can beetles dive?

Yes, beetles can dive. The great diving beetle lives in ponds and lakes and is a fast and fierce hunter. It uses its legs like paddles to dive through the water and catch its food.

Why do ants cut up leaves?

Leafcutter ants cut up small sections of leaves to take back to their nests. The ants then carry the leaves back to a special 'ant' garden where they are stored and used as food for the ants.

Tough bug!

The young of the cranefly or 'daddy long-legs' is called a leather jacket after its tough skin.

Why do moths like the moonlight?

Most moths, such as the Indian moon moth, like moonlight. They use it to search for plant juices such as nectar in flowers. By day they rest in cracks in rocks or among leaves.

Which spider looks like a crab?

Crab spiders look like small crabs with wide bodies and curved legs. They sit on flowers and lie in wait for small insects to grab and eat.

Think

Do you know of any other animals that become active after dark?

Which bug has the most legs?

Centipedes are long and thin, and usually have more than 30 legs. There are more than 3000 types of centipede. Millipedes are even longer and may have up to 100 legs.

Centipede

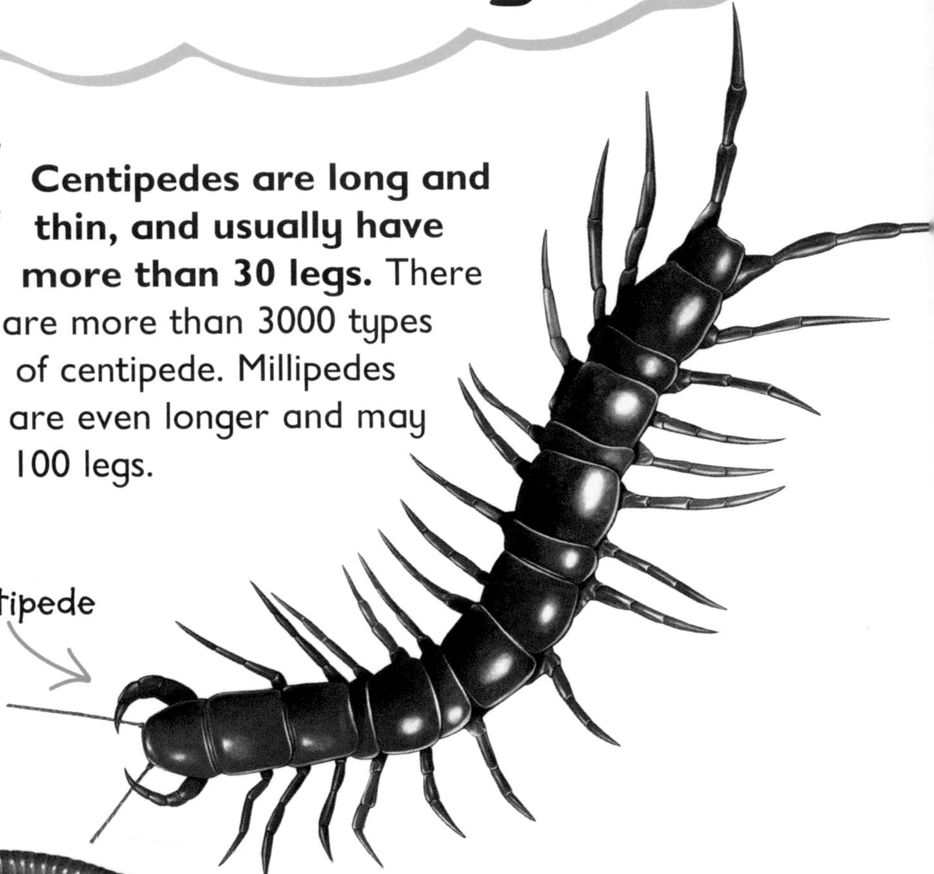

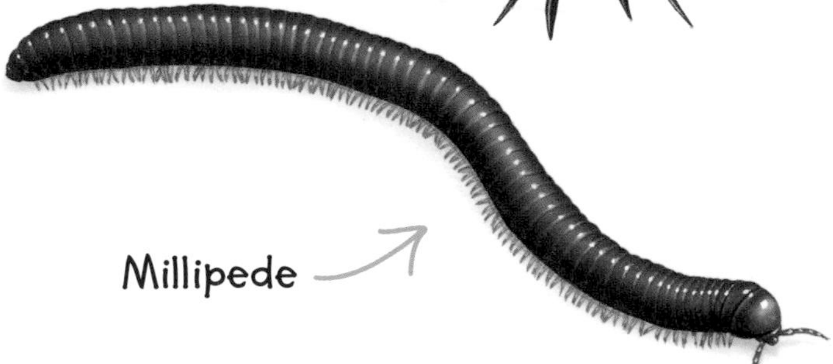

Millipede

Draw

Use brightly coloured pens or pencils and draw your very own crab spider.

What are the greediest insects?

Locusts are a type of grasshopper. They live in dry, warm places. If locusts find a field of crops, they swoop down in large swarms and begin to feast. The whole field can be gone in less than an hour.

Thorny tail

The thorn bug has a hard, pointed body that makes it look like a thorn on a plant.

Can spiders change colour?

Crab spiders hide themselves in flowers and plants so they can catch food. They change colour to match their surroundings so that other insects can't see them. This is called camouflage.

Gold leaf crab spider

Do earwigs really live in ears?

Earwigs don't really crawl into ears or hide in wigs. But they do like dark, damp corners. At night they come out to feed on flower petals, one of their favourite foods.

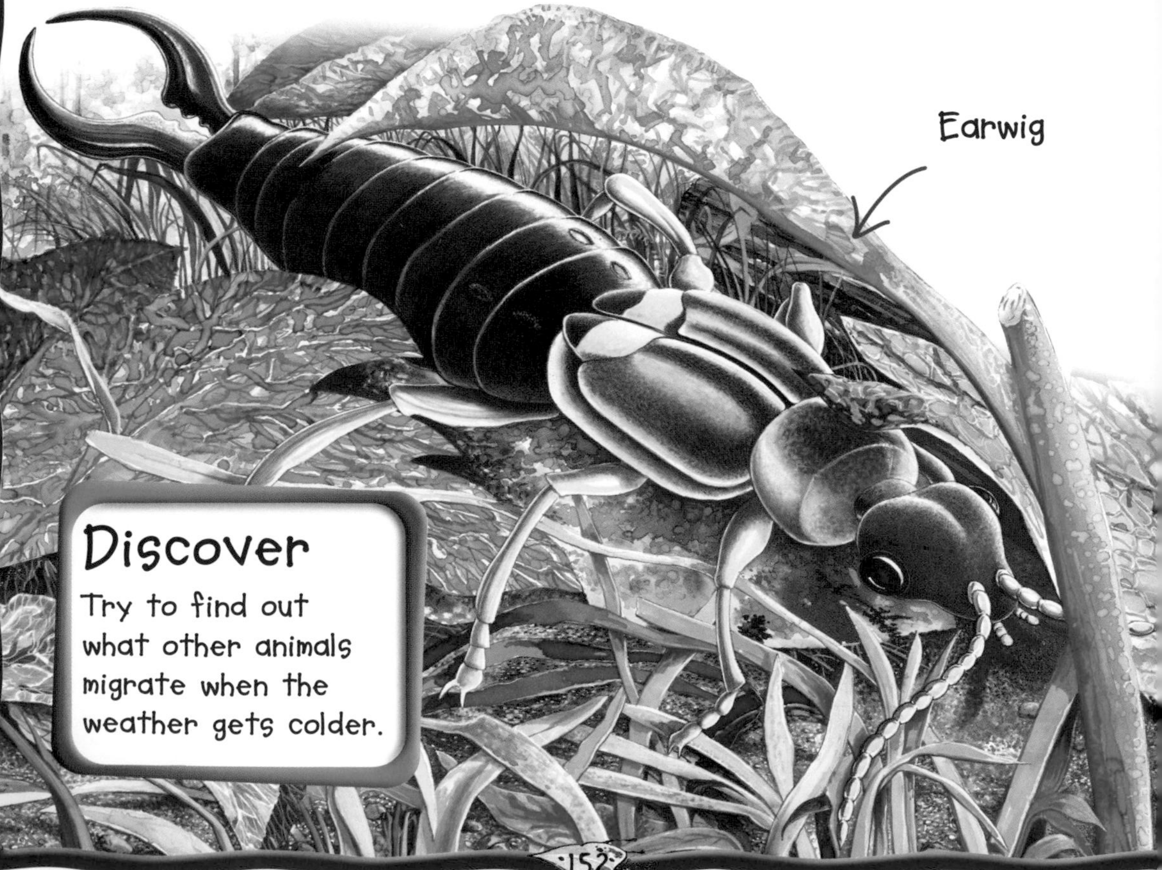

Discover

Try to find out what other animals migrate when the weather gets colder.

How do insects help flowers to grow?

Many insects, including butterflies, visit flowers to collect nectar and pollen. They carry the pollen from flower to flower. This helps flowers form seeds or fruits so that new plants can grow.

Painted lady butterfly

Wonderful webs!

A web-spinning spider makes a new web almost every night – eating the old one to recycle (use again) the silk threads.

Where do insects spend winter?

Some insects travel to warmer lands when the weather gets cold. This is called migration. In North America, monarch butterflies fly south during autumn. They spend the winter in warmer parts of America and fly north again in the spring.

Quiz time

Do you remember what you have read about insects and spiders?

These questions will test your memory. The pictures will help you. If you get stuck, read the pages again.

page 129

1. How many wings does an insect have?

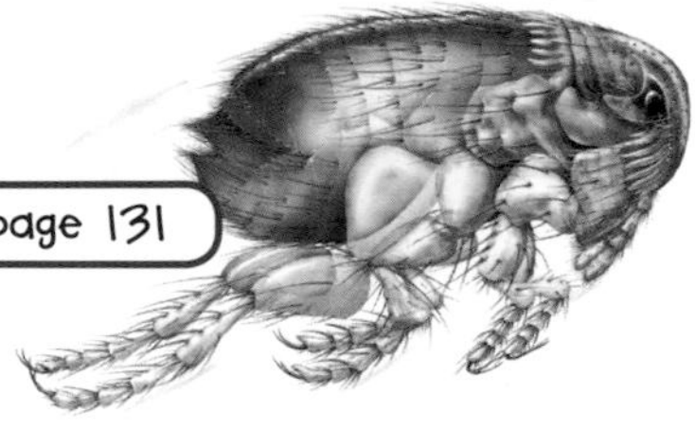

page 131

2. How far can a flea jump?

page 133

3. Can insects walk on water?

page 135

4. How many times can a bee sting you?

page 136

5. Can spiders spit?

6. Do insects like to pray?

page 141

7. Can insects spread disease?

page 141

11. Why do moths like the moonlight?

page 149

8. Why are scorpions' tails so deadly?

page 142

12. Which spider looks like a crab?

page 149

9. What is the deadliest spider?

page 143

13. Which bug has the most legs?

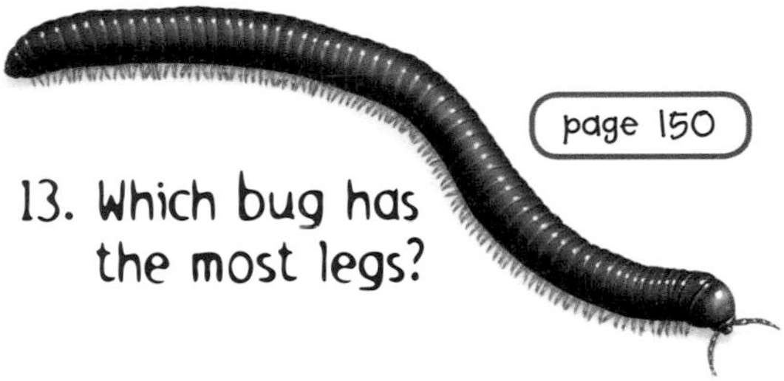

page 150

10. Why do ladybirds have spots?

page 146

Answers

1. Two pairs of wings
2. Over 30 centimetres
3. Yes, the pondskater can
4. A bee can only sting once
5. Yes, the spitting spider can
6. The praying mantis folds its front legs as if it is praying
7. Yes, the mosquito can pass on malaria
8. Their tails have poisonous stings
9. The black widow spider
10. To tell other animals not to eat them
11. It helps them search for food
12. The crab spider
13. The millipede

Questions about...

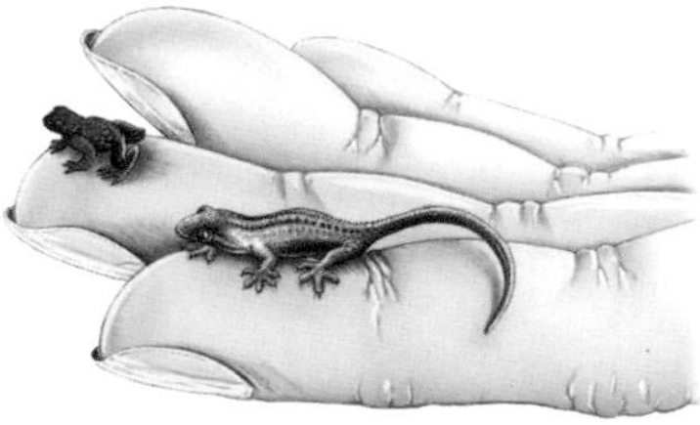

Reptiles & Amphibians

What is a reptile?

Python

Reptiles are cold-blooded animals. This means that they cannot control their body temperature. A reptile's skin is dry and scaly. There are four kinds of reptile – snakes and lizards, crocodiles, tortoises and turtles and the tuatara, a kind of lizard.

Why do reptiles sunbathe?

Reptiles do a lot of sunbathing! This is called basking, and they do this to get warm so that they can move about. When reptiles are cold they find it difficult to move quickly.

Discover

Next time you are on the beach, bury your legs in the sand to feel how cool it is.

What is an amphibian?

Amphibians are cold-blooded animals. Most amphibians live in or around water. The skin of an amphibian is smooth and wet. The main groups of amphibians are frogs and toads, newts and salamanders and caecilians.

Eastern newt

Head in the sand!

Some amphibians, such as the spadefoot toad, live in very hot places. If it gets too hot, the spadefoot toad buries itself in the sand to cool down!

Cane toad

Why do frogs cross the road?

When spring arrives, amphibians come out of hiding. It is time for them to have their babies. Many amphibians return to the pond or stream where they were born. This may mean a very long journey through towns or over busy roads to breeding grounds.

When do amphibians sleep?

When the weather turns cold, amphibians often hide away. They hibernate (go into a deep sleep) under stones and logs. This means that they go to sleep in the autumn, and don't wake up until the next spring!

Mind the frog!

In some places road signs warn drivers that frogs and toads are travelling along the roads to return to their breeding grounds.

Hibernating toad

Can lizards dance?

When the sand gets too hot, the sand lizard of the African Namib Desert performs a strange dance. It lifts its legs up and down off the burning sand or lies on its stomach and raises all its legs at once!

Explore

In the autumn, have a look under some stones and logs for sleeping frogs – try not to wake them!

Why do amphibians lay eggs?

So that their babies can hatch. Amphibians lay eggs in water. Frogs and toads lay a jelly-like string or clump of tiny eggs called spawn. Newts lay one egg at a time. Some amphibians give birth to live young that are born looking like tiny adults.

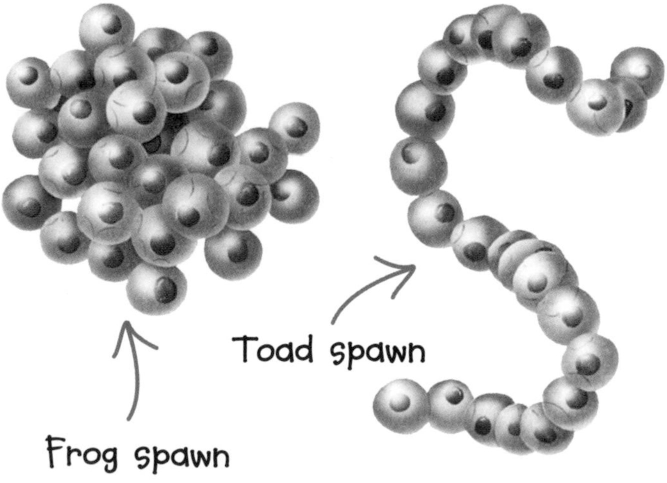

Look

In the spring, look carefully in a pond for frog spawn. Check it each day and you might see it hatch into tadpoles!

Danger in the air!

Frogs and toads have very good hearing. They also have good senses of taste and smell to check for signs of danger in the air around them.

Where do amphibians grow up?

Most amphibians are born and grow up in fresh water such as ponds, pools, streams and rivers. They move onto dry land when they are adults and return to water to have their babies. This is called breeding. Most amphibians completely change their appearance as they grow.

Which toad carries eggs on its back?

The female South American Surinam toad carries her eggs on her back. They are put there by her mate. The eggs stay on the mother's back until they hatch.

Where do reptiles lay their eggs?

Unlike amphibians, most reptiles lay their eggs on land. The eggs feed and protect the young inside them. The egg yolk provides food for the growing young. The shell protects the baby reptile from the outside world.

Crocodile laying eggs

Good luck!

A mother reptile only looks after her babies for a short time. Then they have to look after themselves. They must learn how to look for food and shelter very quickly.

Snake with eggs

Are reptile eggs strong?

Most reptile eggs are much tougher than those of amphibians. This is because they must survive life out of the water. Lizards and snakes lay eggs with leathery shells. Crocodile and tortoise eggs have a hard shell rather like birds' eggs.

Nest

Do baby crocodiles cry?

The baby Nile crocodile makes a very high-pitched noise, as if it's crying, when it is ready to hatch. Its mother then helps the baby to hatch by gently rolling the egg in her mouth.

Remember

Can you remember the two ways that an egg helps the young reptile growing inside it?

Are there tortoises in the desert?

Yes, there are. The desert tortoise is a shy reptile that lives in the sandy deserts of North America. It spends most of its time underground in the cool sand to escape the heat of the Sun. Adult desert tortoises can survive for about a year without water.

Are dragons real?

Early explorers told tales of dragons that lived in faraway lands. It may be that these explorers had seen giant lizards such as the Komodo dragon. These huge reptiles aren't really dragons at all!

Find

The Brazilian frog lives in Brazil in South America. Can you find Brazil on a map?

It's a boy...no!

A male baby alligator will develop in a warm egg, but a female baby alligator will develop in a cooler egg. For crocodiles, it's the other way around!

Can a frog sit on your finger?

One frog could! The Brazilian frog is less than 10 millimetres long and is small enough to sit on your thumbnail! The world's tiniest reptile is a type of lizard called a gecko. This lizard is less than 20 millimetres long.

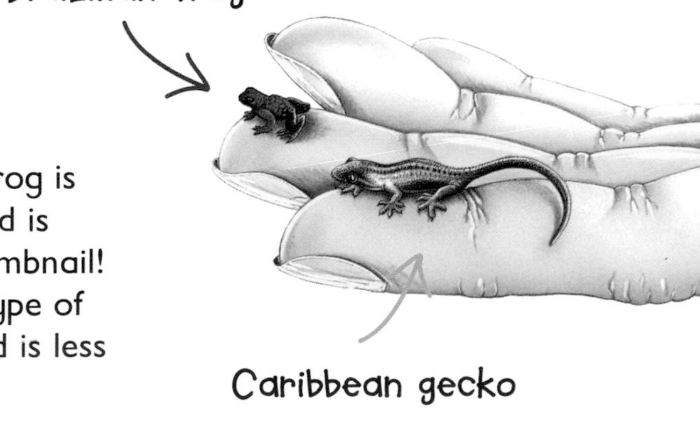

Why do lizards stick to walls?

Geckos can climb up walls or even walk upside down on ceilings. They are able to cling on because they have five wide-spreading toes, each with sticky toe-pads, on each foot. These strong pads are covered with millions of tiny hairs that grip surfaces tightly.

Why do chameleons have long tongues?

So they can catch their dinner. The chameleon keeps very still. When a tasty fly buzzes past, the chameleon catches it by quickly shooting out its long, sticky tongue and pulling the fly into its mouth.

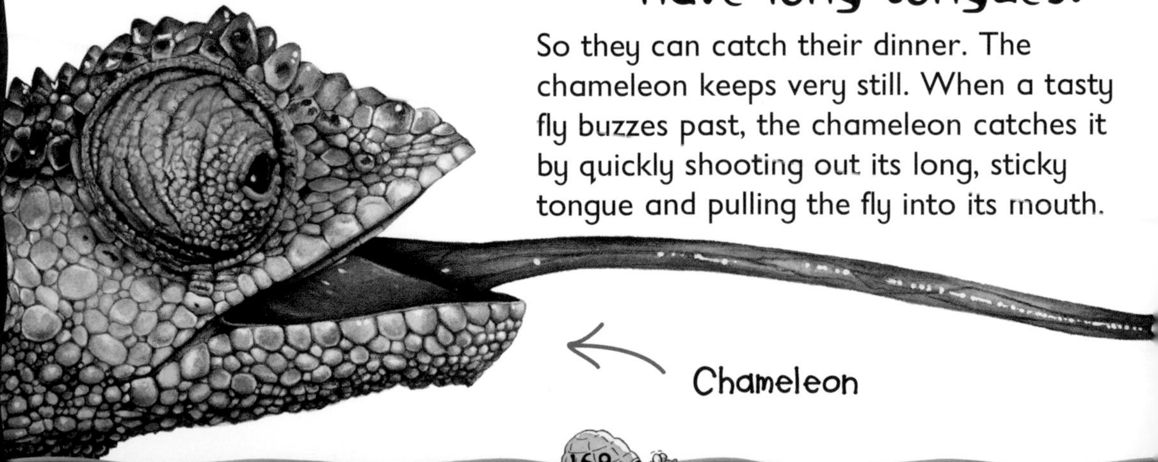

Chameleon

Pretend

Look in the mirror and stick out your tongue – pretend to be a chameleon catching a fly!

Gecko

Which reptile can fly?

Flying geckos have webbed feet and folds of skin along their legs, tail and sides. This means that they can fly, or glide, over short distances. They do this to either catch food, or to escape from danger.

Tight spot!

The chuckwalla lizard gets itself into tight corners. It can jam itself into a crack in a rock, then puff its body up so that enemies cannot pull it out.

Which lizard huffs and puffs?

The male anole lizard guards his home from other lizards in an unusual way. If other males come too close, he puffs out a bright red throat pouch at them. Two males may face each other with puffy throats for hours at a time!

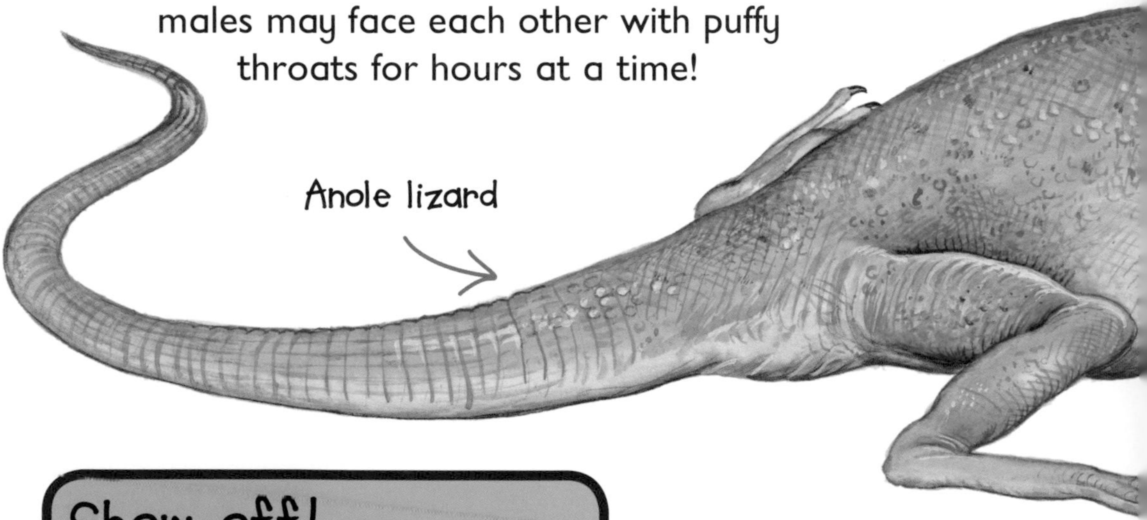

Show off!

A male newt goes to great lengths to impress a female during the mating season. He often has brightly coloured skin, which he shows off to her!

Are lizards frilly?

The frilled lizard can be! This reptile has a large flap of skin that normally lies flat around its neck. When faced with danger, it spreads this skin out to form a huge, stiff neck frill that makes it look bigger and scarier!

Frilled lizard

Why do lizards show off their muscles?

Some male agamid lizards try to impress females with a little body-building. They can be seen perched on top of rocks, doing push-ups and bobbing their heads up and down.

Think

Can you think of any other animals that have brightly coloured skin, fur or feathers?

Why do snakes stick out their tongues?

Snakes have poor hearing and eyesight. They use their tongue to 'smell' the air for food or danger by constantly flicking it in and out. Rattlesnakes can sense heat given off by their prey, even in the dark.

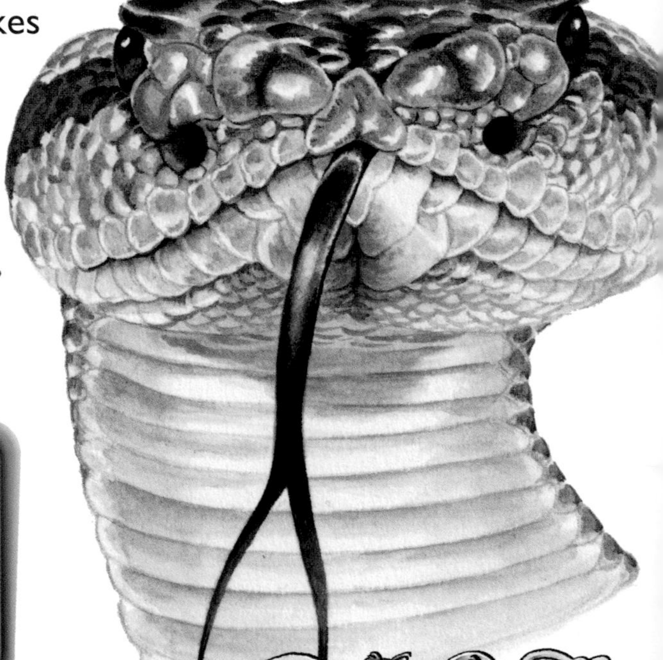

Rattlesnake

Count

Try to stare at something without blinking. Count how many seconds go by before you need to blink.

Can you see through a gecko?

One African gecko has very thin skin covering its ears. If you were to look at it with its ears lined up, you would be able to see light coming through from the other side of its head!

Strong shell!

A giant tortoise is so big and strong that it can support a one tonne weight. This means that it could support a small car!

Why can't iguanas blink?

Iguanas have very big eyes and good eyesight, but they cannot blink. Unlike humans, iguanas don't have moveable eyelids. Instead of shutting their eyes to blink, they have special clear eyelids that sweep over their eyes to clean them.

Why do snakes squeeze their food?

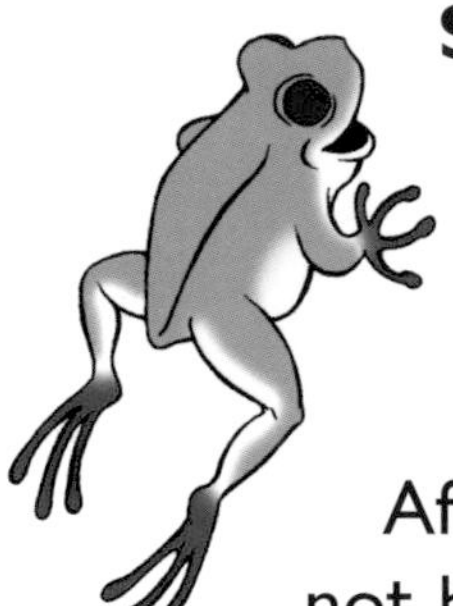

Some snakes, like this ratsnake, kill their prey by squeezing it. They wrap their bodies around their meal and squeeze tightly until it stops breathing. Then the snake swallows the prey whole. After a big meal, the snake will not be hungry for a long time.

Can reptiles live underground?

Some reptiles slither below the ground. In hot places, some snakes burrow down into the sand to escape the Sun's fierce heat. The caecilian burrows through the mud of its tropical homeland, searching for worms to eat.

Measure

Using a tape measure, cut a piece of string 10 metres long. How many times could a royal python wrap around you?

Which snake changes colour?

The milksnake pretends to be the coral snake by changing colour. This is because the milksnake is not dangerous to bigger animals, but the coral snake is. Predators will not try to eat the coral snake because they are afraid of being bitten.

Ratsnake

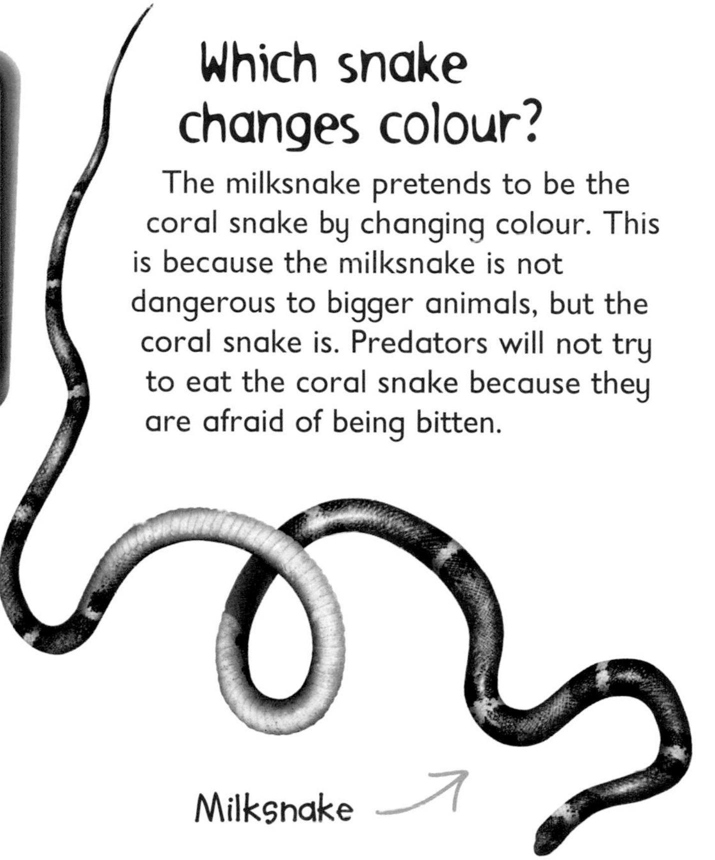

Milksnake

King of snakes!

The longest snake in the world is the royal python, which grows up to 10 metres long. It could wrap its body around a person 12 times!

Which snake writes in the sand?

The sidewinding viper lives in the deserts of the United States. It moves along by pushing its body sideways against the sand, leaving a series of marks that are shaped like sideways letter Js. It does this so that its belly is not on the hot sand for too long.

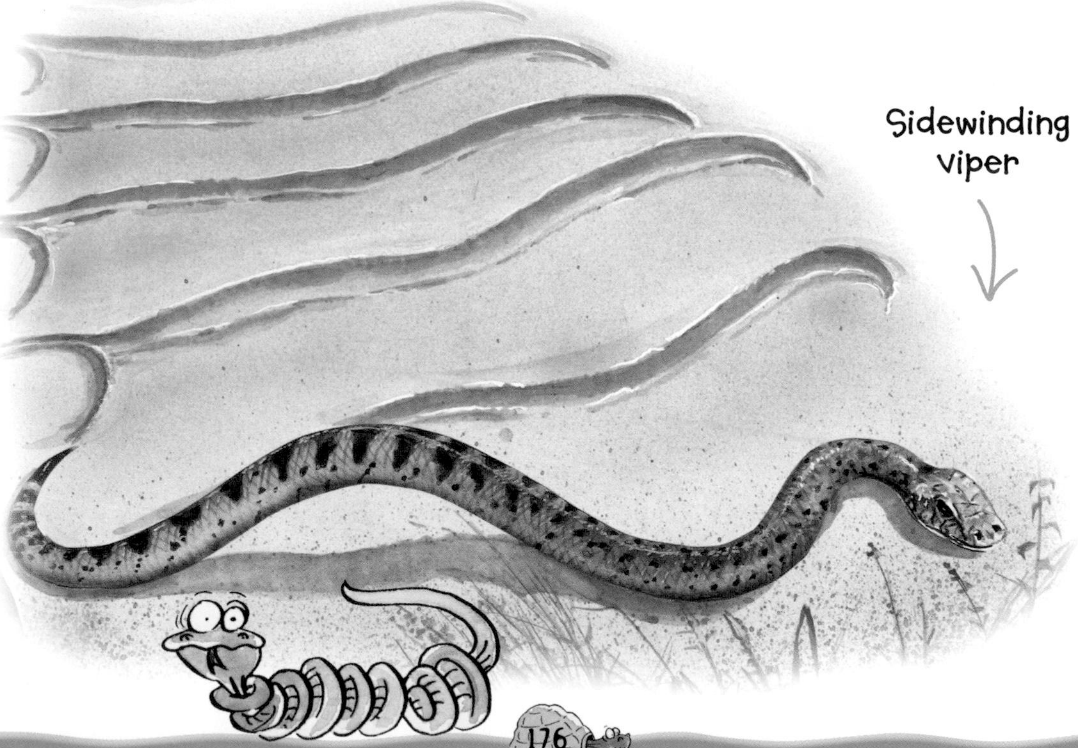

Sea turtle

Why do turtles swim so far?

To have their babies. Every two or three years, sea turtles may swim 1000 kilometres to the beaches where they hatched to lay their eggs. Sea turtles have light, flat shells so they can swim easily under water.

Giants of the sea!

The largest turtle in the sea is called the leatherback turtle. It is 2 metres long – what a giant!

Can snakes live in water?

The floating sea snake can. Some fish swim close to the floating sea snake's tail to avoid being eaten. When the snake fancies a snack, it swims backwards, fooling the unlucky fish into thinking its head is its tail!

Swim

When you next go swimming, try to swim backwards like a sea snake. Ask an adult to help you.

Are frogs dangerous?

Some are! Even one lick of the poison arrow frog would make a predator very ill. Its brightly coloured skin warns enemies that it is poisonous and dangerous to eat.

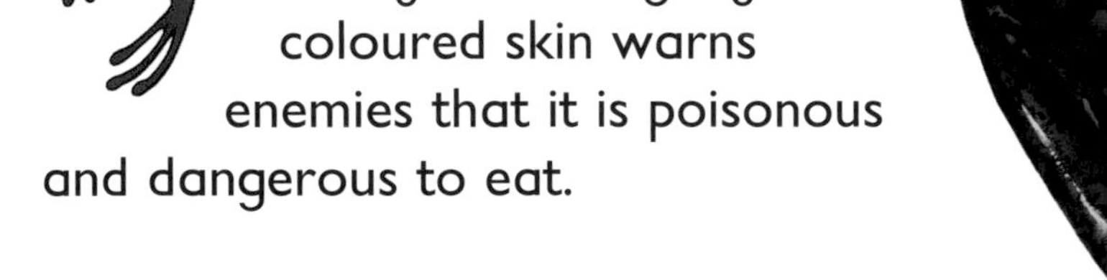

Can a lizard's tail fall off?

Some lizards have detachable tails! If a hungry hunter grabs the tail of a five-lined tree skink lizard, it will be left just holding a twitching tail. The lizard can quickly run away and will grow back a new tail.

Think

Can you remember how long it takes a snake to shed all of its skin?

Poison arrow frog

Why do snakes shed their skin?

A snake's skin does not grow with its body. This means that it has to shed its old skin as it grows bigger. It can take about two weeks for a snake to shed its skin completely.

Grass snake shedding skin

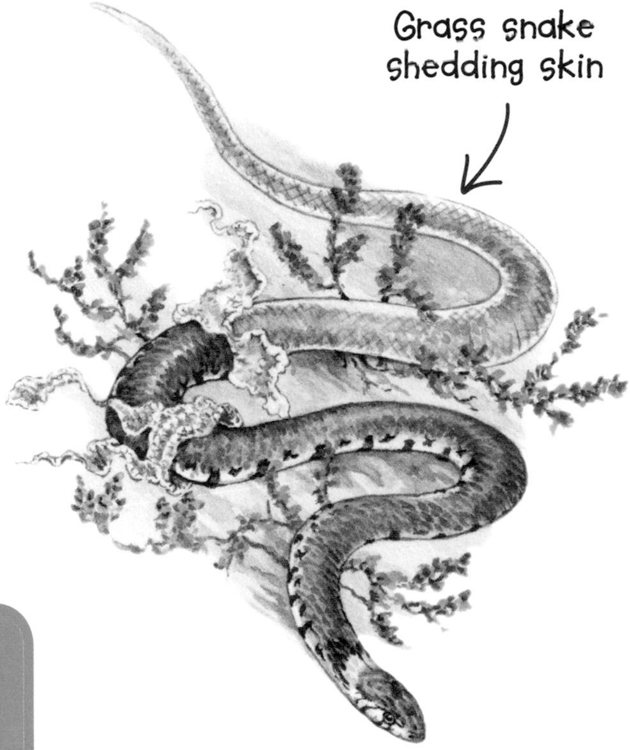

Ready to burst!

A snake has to swallow food whole as it can't chew. It opens its jaws extra wide to gulp down animals much larger than itself.

Which lizard can run on two legs?

The crested water dragon from Asia can. In an emergency, this lizard can stand up on its back legs to run away from enemies. This is because it has large back feet and can run faster on two legs than on four over short distances.

Sneaky hunters!

Crocodiles and alligators wait in shallow water for animals to come and drink, then they leap up and drag them under the water.

Are toads colourful?

The fire-bellied toad has a bright red tummy. When it is threatened, the toad leaps away to safety, and the quick flash of red confuses its attacker and gives the frog more time to escape.

Play

How easy is it to sneak up on someone? See how quietly you can creep around the house without being noticed.

Do turtles play tricks?

The alligator snapper turtle looks like a rock as it lies on the ocean floor. The tip of its tongue looks like a juicy worm, which it waves at passing prey to tempt them into its jaws.

Do reptiles eat amphibians?

Some do. Most reptiles are meat eaters. The dwarf crocodile is so small that one frog is a big dinner. Frogs can jump very fast, but the dwarf crocodile snaps quickly at anything that makes a splash in the water near its jaws.

Are crocodiles always hungry?

After a big meal, a crocodile may not feel hungry again for a month or two. One of the most dangerous reptiles is the Nile crocodile. Each year it kills more people in Africa than lions do.

Think

How many different animals can you think of that have long, powerful tails?

Old lizard!

Some crocodiles are very old indeed. They can live to be over 100 years old. Crocodiles continue to grow throughout their lives.

Can crocodiles walk on their tails?

If they are being threatened, crocodiles can move so fast that they almost leap out of the water. This is called 'tail-walking'. Their tails are long and powerful, and they can kill with a single swipe.

Nile crocodiles

Quiz time

Do you remember what you have read about reptiles and amphibians? These questions will test your memory. The pictures will help you. If you get stuck, read the pages again.

page 158

1. What is a reptile?

2. What is an amphibian?

page 159

3. Which toad carries eggs on its back?

page 163

4. Where do reptiles lay their eggs?

page 164

page 168

5. Why do chameleons have long tongues?

6. Why do lizards show off their muscles?

page 171

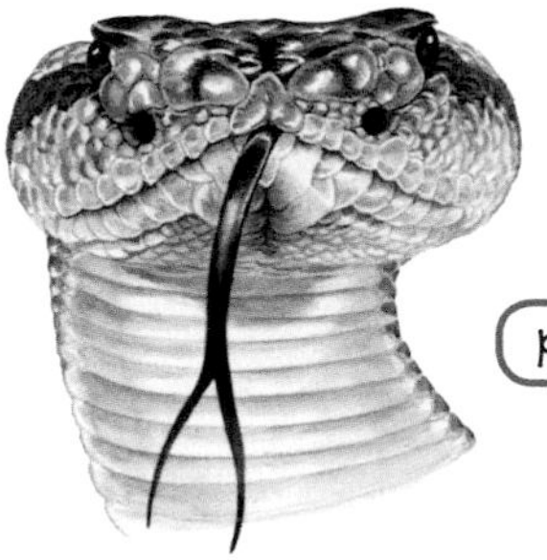

page 172

7. Why do snakes stick out their tongues?

page 173

8. Why can't iguanas blink?

9. Can snakes live in water?

page 177

10. Are frogs dangerous?

page 178

11. Can a lizard's tail fall off?

page 178

12. Which lizard can run on two legs?

page 180

13. Are crocodiles always hungry?

page 183

Answers

1. A cold-blooded animal with dry and scaly skin
2. A cold-blooded animal with wet and smooth skin
3. The female South American Surinam toad
4. On land
5. So they can catch their dinner
6. So they can impress females
7. To 'smell' the air for food or danger
8. Because their eyelids do not move
9. Yes, the floating sea snakes lives in water
10. The poison arrow frog is very dangerous
11. The five-lined tree skink lizard's tail can
12. The crested water dragon from Asia
13. No. After a big meal, a crocodile may not feel hungry for a month or two

Questions about...

Birds

What is special about birds?

Birds can fly, walk, run and even swim! Because they have wings, birds are able to fly to all parts of the world, from steamy rainforests to the icy Arctic. There are about 9000 different types of bird, from beautiful barn owls to giant ostriches.

Do birds have teeth?

Birds don't have teeth. Instead, they have really strong mouths that are called beaks, or bills. Sharp, pointed beaks are good for grabbing bugs and short, strong beaks are great for cracking nuts open!

Discover

Beaks and feathers are made of a special tough material. See if you can you discover what it's called.

The early bird!

The oldest-known bird lived about 150 million years ago. Archaeopteryx (ark-ee-op-ter-ix) had feathers and wings, but it had teeth instead of a beak.

Why do birds lay eggs?

Birds lay eggs so that their babies can grow. Baby birds are called chicks and they begin life in an egg. The eggs are kept safe in a nest until they hatch.

How do birds fly?

Birds can fly because they have wings, powerful muscles and very light bones. Feathers also help birds move smoothly through the air. This peregrine falcon is the fastest of all animals. It can reach top speeds of 180 kilometres an hour as it swoops and dives.

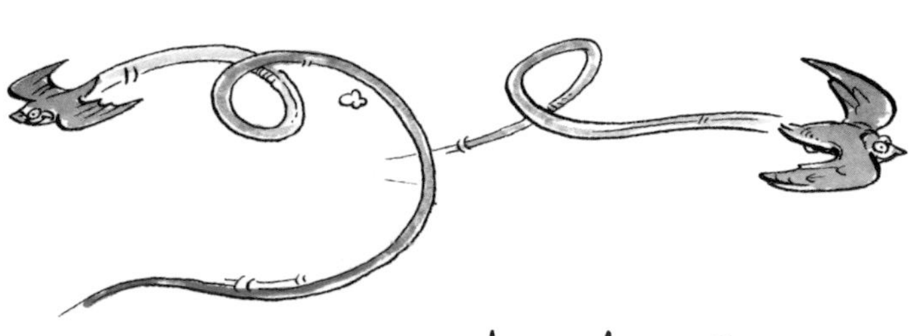

How far can a bird fly?

Birds can fly very long distances. Swifts are super fliers and even eat and mate while they swoop through the clouds. When young swifts leave the nest they may fly for the next two years and travel more than 500,000 kilometres!

Count

If a bird beats its wings ten times in one second, how many times would it beat its wings in two seconds?

Do all birds fly?

All birds have wings, but not all of them fly. This speedy roadrunner lives in the desert. It can fly, but it prefers to walk or run as it looks for lizards, snakes and bugs in the sand.

Roadrunner

Swift

Hum that tune!

Hummingbirds beat their wings 50 times a second. As the wings slice through the air they make the humming noise that gives the birds their name.

Why are some birds colourful?

Birds can be big show-offs and they use bright colours to make themselves look attractive. Male birds are usually more colourful than females. When this peacock sees a female (a peahen) he displays his fine tail and shakes it, so she can admire his great beauty.

Love birds!

Great crested grebes are water birds that dance for each other. During the dance they offer each other gifts – beakfuls of water weed. Lovely!

Peacock

Which birds strut around and coo?

Male birds puff up their feathers, strut around and make cooing noises to impress the females. These cocks-of-the-rocks also dance and spread their wings to show off to the female birds. They live in the South American rainforest.

Cocks-of-the-rocks

Why do birds sing?

Birds sing to get the attention of other birds. Like their colourful feathers, they may use songs to attract mates. Some birds squawk loudly if they are being attacked. Most baby birds learn to sing by copying their parents.

Dress-up

A bird's feathers are called its plumage. Put on some bright clothes and see if anyone notices your plumage!

Why do birds lay eggs in nests?

Birds lay their eggs in a nest to keep them safe. Once the eggs have hatched, the little chicks stay in the nest until they have grown enough to be able to fly. These bald eagles build giant nests up to 2.5 metres across.

Why are cuckoos lazy?

Cuckoos don't bother making their own nests. Instead, they lay their eggs in other birds' nests. This way cuckoos do not have all the hard work of looking after their own chicks – other birds do it for them!

Make it

Use sticks and twigs to make a nest. Make a soft lining with grass or straw. Pop some chocolate eggs in the middle.

How do birds build nests?

Birds build their nests in different ways, but most of them use twigs and sticks. African weaver birds make their delicate nests using strips of leaves and grass. They knot and weave the strips together to make a cosy, safe home.

1. The weaver bird twists strips of leaves

2. The roof is made

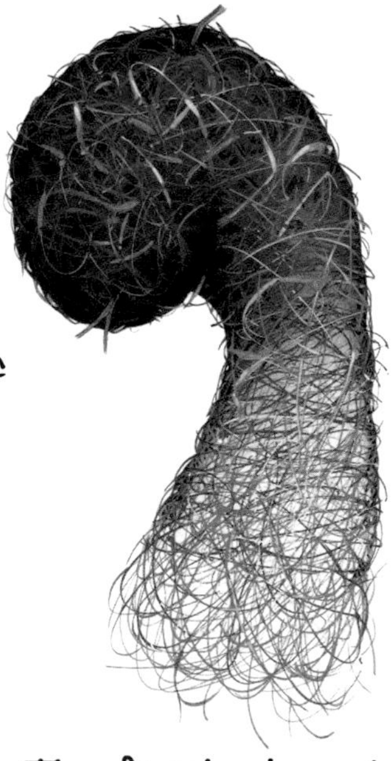

3. The finished nest

Watch the birdie!

Most birds take minutes to lay an egg. The mother cuckoo can lay an egg in 9 seconds! This allows her to quickly pop it in the nest of another bird.

What is a bird of prey?

Birds of prey are hunting birds. As they soar and glide across the sky they search for animals to eat. Golden eagles have extremely good eyesight and can spot food far away. They swoop to the ground and grab rabbits and mice with their sharp claws.

Top bird!

Eagles like to build their nests in high places. One pair of sea eagles made their nest on top of a light-tower by the coast in Norway!

How does a sea eagle catch fish?

Sea eagles need good eyes and strong claws to catch a swimming fish. Each foot has a pointed hook for holding onto a slippery fish. Sea eagles take their fish to a cliff or rocky ledge where they can eat in comfort.

Sea eagle

Do hunting birds live in towns?

It's unusual to see big hunting birds such as eagles in towns. But you might see smaller ones, such as ravens. These black birds are very clever animals. They hunt mice and rats but they will eat almost any food that they can find.

Try it

Eagles use their feet to grab their food. See if you can pick up anything using just your feet.

Why do woodpeckers peck?

Woodpeckers peck at trees to disturb the little insects that live in the bark. They then gobble them up. These birds can also use their strong, pointed beaks to hammer at the tree until they have made a hole big enough for a nest.

Hummm, I'm hungry!

Bee hummingbirds beat their wings 200 times a second. If we used up the same amount of energy we would need to eat three times our own weight in potatoes each day!

How do honeyguides find their food?

Honeyguide birds follow honey badgers to find their favourite food – delicious bee grubs! The clever birds follow the badgers when they go in search of a bee's nest. When the badger opens the nest it feeds on the honey, while the birds eat the grubs and beeswax.

Make it

Ask an adult to help you make a bird feeder. You can then hang it upside down from a tree.

Do antbirds eat ants?

Antbirds follow army ants as they march through the forest, but they don't usually eat them. The birds perch on trees as the army ants pass by, then they pounce on the other small animals and insects that come to feed on the ants.

How does a bird eat a snail?

Birds that eat snails need to get the soft body out of the hard shell. Some birds smash snails against rocks. This snail kite uses its sharp beak to cut the slimy snail away from its shell and hook it out.

Snail kite

Knobbly knees!

Flamingos look as if they have got back-to-front legs. Actually, what appear to be their knees are really their ankles!

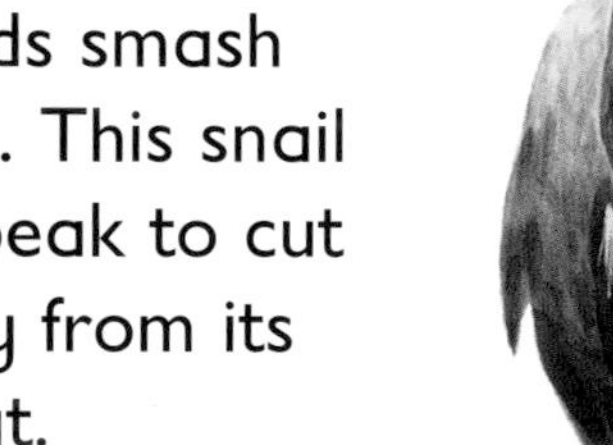

Which bird has a scissor-shaped beak?

The beak of a skimmer is shaped like scissors. This is because the lower beak is much longer and flatter than the top beak. As it flies over water, the skimmer dips its lower beak below the surface. When it touches a fish it snaps its beak shut.

Why do flamingos have long necks?

Flamingos have long necks so that they can reach underwater to find their food. They use their beaks to catch tiny pink creatures called shrimps that float past. Flamingos turn pink after eating lots of these shrimps!

Remember

Can you remember what a skimmer's beak is shaped like? If you can't, read this page again to find out.

Quiz time

Do you remember what you have read about birds?

These questions will test your memory. The pictures will help you. If you get stuck, read the pages again.

page 189

1. Why do birds lay eggs?

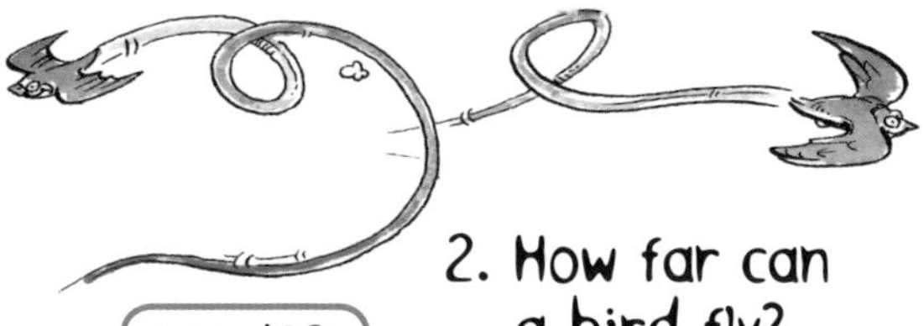

page 190

2. How far can a bird fly?

3. Do all birds fly?

page 191

4. Why do birds sing?

page 193

5. How do birds build nests?

page 195

6. Why are cuckoos lazy?

page 195

7. What is a bird of prey?

page 196

11. How does a bird eat a snail?

page 200

page 197

8. Do hunting birds live in towns?

12. Which bird has a scissor-shaped beak?

page 201

page 201

page 198

9. Why do woodpeckers peck?

13. Why do flamingos have long necks?

10. Do antbirds eat ants?

page 199

Answers

1. So their babies can grow
2. Very long distances
3. Not all birds can fly
4. To get the attention of other birds
5. With twigs and sticks
6. Because they don't make their own nests
7. A hunting bird
8. Smaller ones do
9. To disturb insects that live in the bark
10. Yes, they eat army ants
11. The snail kite hooks it out with its beak
12. The skimmer
13. So they can reach underwater to find their food

Questions about...

Mammals

Why are some animals furry?

Fur or hair keeps some animals warm. Animals that have fur or hair are called mammals. Fur also protects from the weather. This hairy orang-utan lives in the rainforest. She picks fruit and leaves to eat. She feeds her baby on milk.

What is a joey?

A joey is a baby kangaroo. When a joey is born it is smaller than your big toe! Even though it is tiny and blind, the joey crawls all the way to its mother's pouch and climbs in. It feeds on milk from its mother.

Egg-citing news!

Most mammals give birth. This means that they have babies, cubs or kittens. Some strange mammals, such as the duck-billed platypus, lay eggs.

Find out

Were you a beautiful baby, or did you hatch from an egg? Look at old photos of yourself to find out.

Why do some mammals sniff the air?

Many mammals use their noses to get information about the world around them. Their noses are very sensitive to smells. Wild animals, such as deer and rabbits, sniff the air around them to check for signs of danger.

What is the biggest mammal?

The blue whale is – and it's enormous! In fact, it is the biggest animal that has ever lived. Even a baby blue whale is huge – it measures 7 metres in length. All whales are mammals and give birth to their babies, which are called calves.

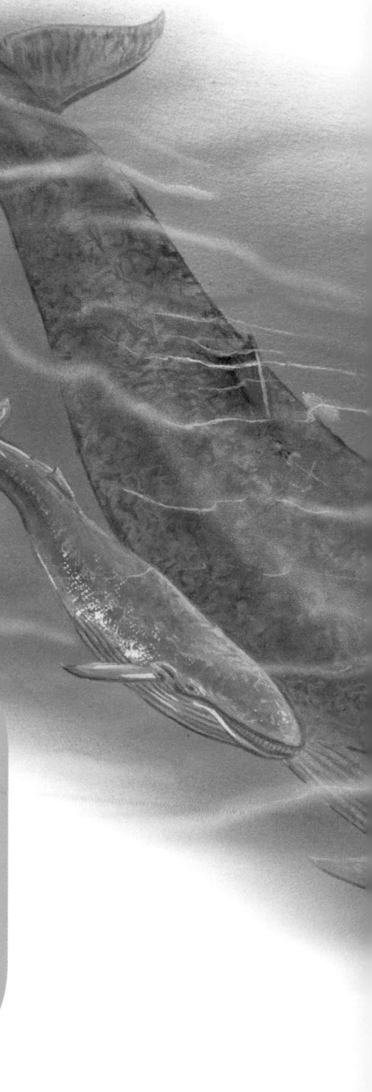

What a hooter!

African elephants have the longest noses! Their noses are called trunks and they can be 2.5 metres long. Trunks are used for smelling, picking up food and drinking.

How big is an elephant?

One African elephant can weigh more than 100 people put together. Elephants are the biggest animals that live on land and they can reach 4 metres in height. They spend most of their day eating to keep themselves that huge!

African elephant

Measure

Using a measuring tape, see if you can mark out how long a blue whale calf is.

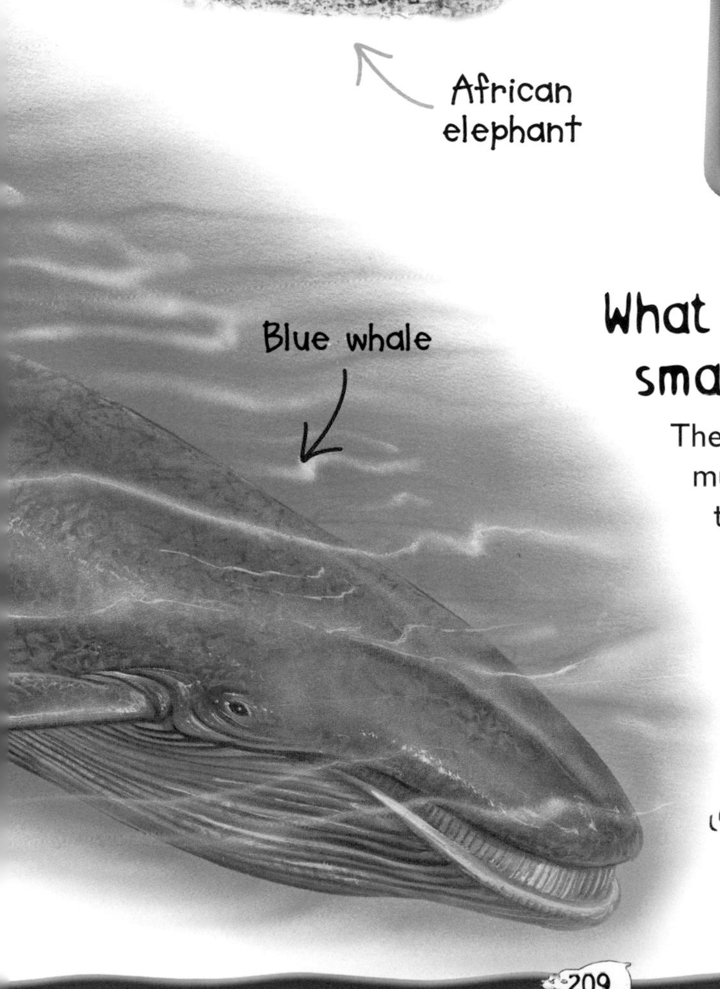

What is the smallest mammal?

The tiny hog-nosed bat is not much bigger than your thumb! Bats are the only mammals that can fly. They usually sleep during the day and come out at night to look for food.

How do cheetahs run so fast?

Cheetahs have big muscles in their legs and they can run faster than any other animal. These speedy cats run out of breath quickly. This means that the animals they're chasing, such as gazelles, often manage to escape. Cheetahs can reach speeds of 100 kilometres an hour!

Hare

Why do hares kick?

Hares sometimes kick out at their enemies. Other animals such as foxes try to catch hares to eat them. If the hare sees, smells or hears an enemy, it can run fast to get away, or kick out with its back legs.

Run

How fast can you run? Ask an adult to time you next time you are in the park or garden.

Whoosh!

The pronghorn deer is one of the fastest mammals in North America. It runs fast to escape from wolves, which hunt it for food.

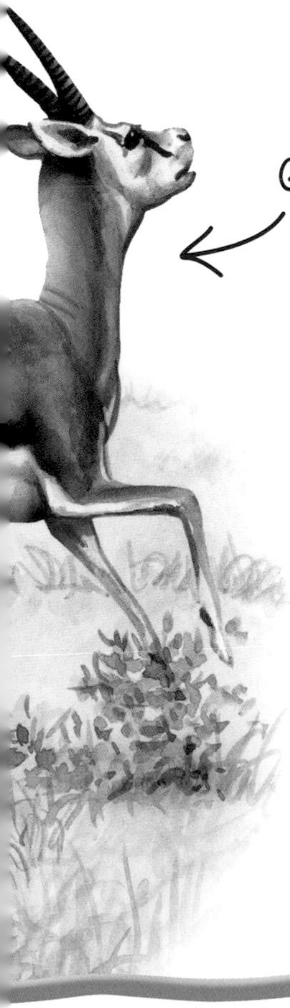

Gazelle

Which mammal is very bouncy?

Kangaroos bounce instead of running. The red kangaroo is a champion jumper and it leaps across the dry deserts of its Australian home. It travels quickly to search for water and food, which are hard to find in a desert.

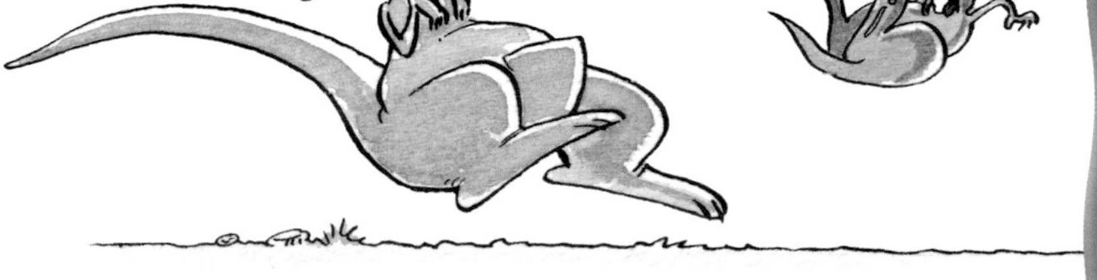

Are mammals good swimmers?

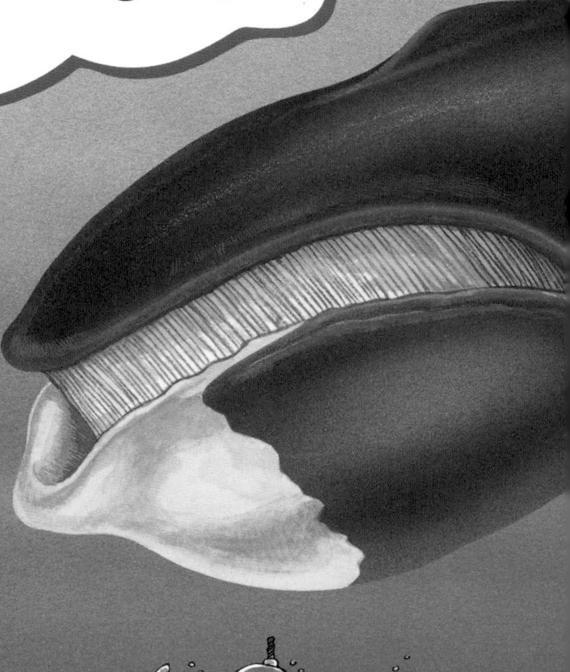

Some mammals are super swimmers! Whales, dolphins and seals have bodies that are perfectly shaped for moving through water smoothly and quickly. They have fins and tails instead of arms and legs. Whales and dolphins spend their whole lives in water.

Harp seal

Can seals breathe underwater?

No mammals can breathe underwater – not even seals, whales and dolphins. Instead, they have to take in all the air they need when they are at the surface of the water, then hold their breath. Some seals can stay underwater for an hour at a time!

Diving deep!

The Weddell seal is a daring diver. It plunges down to the deep, dark, cold water of the oceans as it hunts for fish to eat.

What does a killer whale kill?

Killer whales kill squid, fish, seals and even birds. They are strong swimmers and have sharp, pointed teeth. Killer whales can be friendly. They live in family groups and calves stay with their mothers all their lives!

Swim

You are a mammal and you can learn to swim too! Visit your local pool for some watery fun!

Are polar bears cuddly?

Polar bears may look cuddly with their thick, white fur, but they are fierce hunters. These bears live in the ice-covered lands near the North Pole. Their fur keeps them warm – they even have fur on the soles of their feet so that their toes don't get frost bite!

Polar bear

Lots of lemmings!

A female lemming can have her first babies when she is only 14 days old. From then on, she can have as many as 12 babies every single month!

Why are some animals white?

White animals usually live in places that are covered with snow in winter. A white Arctic hare blends into the snow and hides from enemies. In summer, the snow melts and the hare grows brown fur.

Paint

Paint a snowy scene showing some animals that live in cold places, such as polar bears, seals and penguins.

How do seals stay warm?

Seals spend a lot of their time underwater in cold parts of the world. They can keep warm because they have thick layers of fat, called blubber, under their skin. Seals also have waterproof fur that stops water getting through to their skin.

Why do wolves live in packs?

Wolves live in packs because they hunt together and look after one another. A mother wolf takes good care of her cubs. As the cubs grow, they are brought food from their father and other members of the wolf pack.

Cool cats!

Lions may be fierce, but they are also very lazy. They sleep or doze for more than 20 hours a day, keeping cool in the shade!

How many meerkats live together?

Meerkats live in groups of up to 30 animals. A group is called a colony and each colony is made up of several families. While some meerkats search for food, others stand guard and look for enemies, such as hawks.

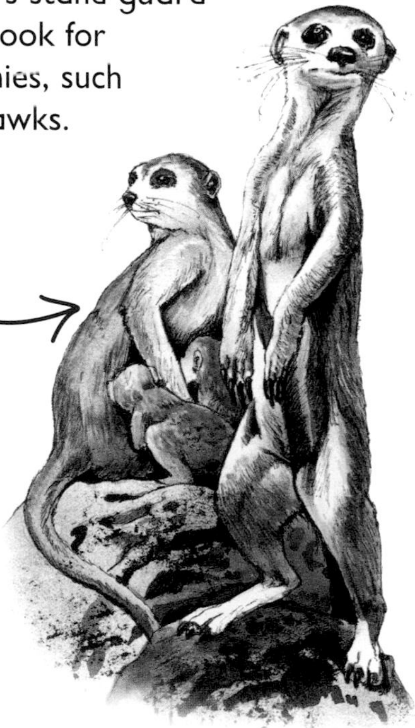

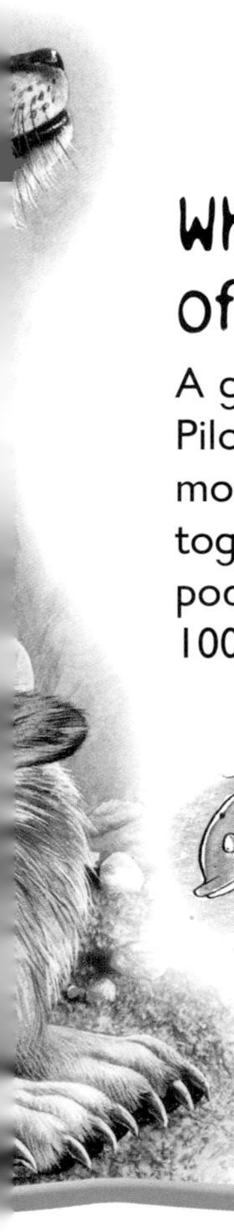

What is a group of whales called?

A group of whales is called a pod. Pilot whales live in pods of 20 or more animals that swim and hunt together. Some dolphins live in pods that may have more than 1000 members.

Count

How many people can you count in your family? Include all your grandparents, aunts, uncles and cousins.

How big is a baby panda?

Pandas give birth to tiny babies, or cubs. Each cub could fit inside your hand and weighs the same as an apple. Newborn pandas are blind and helpless. They do not open their eyes until they are two or three months old.

What are baby elephants called?

Baby elephants are called calves. Soon after they are born, elephant calves are able to stand up. Within a few days, they can run around. Elephants live in groups called herds. The adult elephants protect the young from lions and hyenas.

Elephant calf

Big baby!

The baby blue whale is bigger than any other mammal baby. It weighs more than 30 people put together and drinks up to 500 litres of milk every day.

Measure

How much milk do you drink every day? Use a measuring jug to see how much milk fills up a glass.

Which mammal has the most babies at a time?

The Virginia opossum can have up to 21 babies at a time – more than any other mammal. Each baby opossum is no bigger than a fingertip! If it is attacked, a Virginia opossum lies down and pretends to be dead.

How do tigers catch their food?

Tigers are hunters. Their bodies are perfect for finding, chasing and killing other animals. Stripy fur helps the tiger blend in with tall grass so they are difficult to spot. When a tiger sees a meal, it runs and pounces. It uses its claws and teeth to kill.

What do bears eat?

Bears eat all kinds of food. Some bears hunt other animals but most eat insects, fruit and leaves. Sloth bears love to eat termites. They have long claws for digging out termite nests. The bears suck the termites up one at a time!

Great apes!

Chimpanzees live in groups that hunt together. They search for other monkeys, birds and antelopes to eat. They also form groups that attack other groups of chimpanzees.

Sloth bear

Why do dogs hunt in packs?

Wild dogs hunt in packs because they are more likely to get something to eat. By working together they can surround an animal. They may catch a bigger animal than one dog alone could catch.

Work

Working together is best. True or false? Help an adult with the shopping or the housework to find out!

Are rhinos dangerous?

A rhinoceros is one of the most dangerous mammals. Mother rhinos may attack people, or other animals, to protect their babies. They can run fast and they have sharp horns for attacking. Male rhinos also use their horns to fight one another.

Bee-eaters!

Smelly skunks sometimes feed on bees. They roll the bees on the ground to remove the stings before eating them.

Why do some mammals have scales?

Some mammals have scales to protect themselves, rather like a suit of armour. Pangolins are strange ant-eating mammals that live in Africa and Asia. Their bodies are covered in overlapping scales that protect them from other animals – and the stinging bites of ants.

Pangolin

Rhinoceros

What is the stinkiest mammal?

Skunks are very stinky mammals! These stripy creatures shake their tails at an enemy to warn it to stay away. If that doesn't work, the skunk raises its tail and sprays a smelly liquid in its enemy's face!

Make it

Ask an adult to help you make a cardboard suit of armour. How easy is it to move wearing the armour?

Quiz time

Do you remember what you have read about mammals?

These questions will test your memory. The pictures will help you. If you get stuck, read the pages again.

1. What is a joey?

page 207

2. What is the biggest mammal?

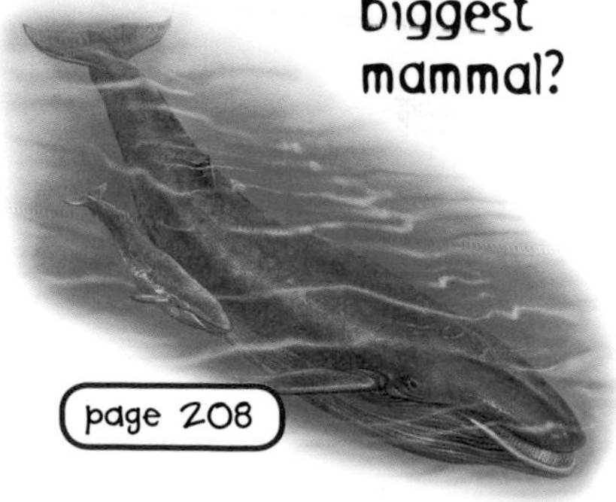

page 208

3. Which mammal is very bouncy?

page 211

4. Can seals breathe underwater?

page 212

5. Are polar bears cuddly?

page 214

6. Why are some animals white?

page 215

7. Why do wolves live in packs?

page 216

page 221

11. What do bears eat?

8. How many meerkats live together?

page 217

page 221

12. Why do dogs hunt in packs?

13. Are rhinos dangerous?

page 222

9. How big is a baby panda?

page 218

page 219

10. What are baby elephants called?

Answers

1. A baby kangaroo
2. The blue whale
3. The kangaroo
4. No
5. No, they are fierce hunters
6. To blend in with their surroundings
7. Because they hunt together and look after each other
8. Up to 30
9. As big as your hand
10. Calves
11. Insects, fruit and leaves
12. They are more likely to get something to eat
13. Yes, rhinos are one of the most dangerous animals

Questions about...

Ancient Egypt

Why were the pyramids built?

Pyramids were tombs (burial places) for Egyptian rulers, called pharaohs. The three great pyramids of Khufu, Khafre and Menkaure were built in Giza, Egypt, 4500 years ago. The Great Pyramid of Khufu is the biggest. It took 20 years and 4000 workers to build it!

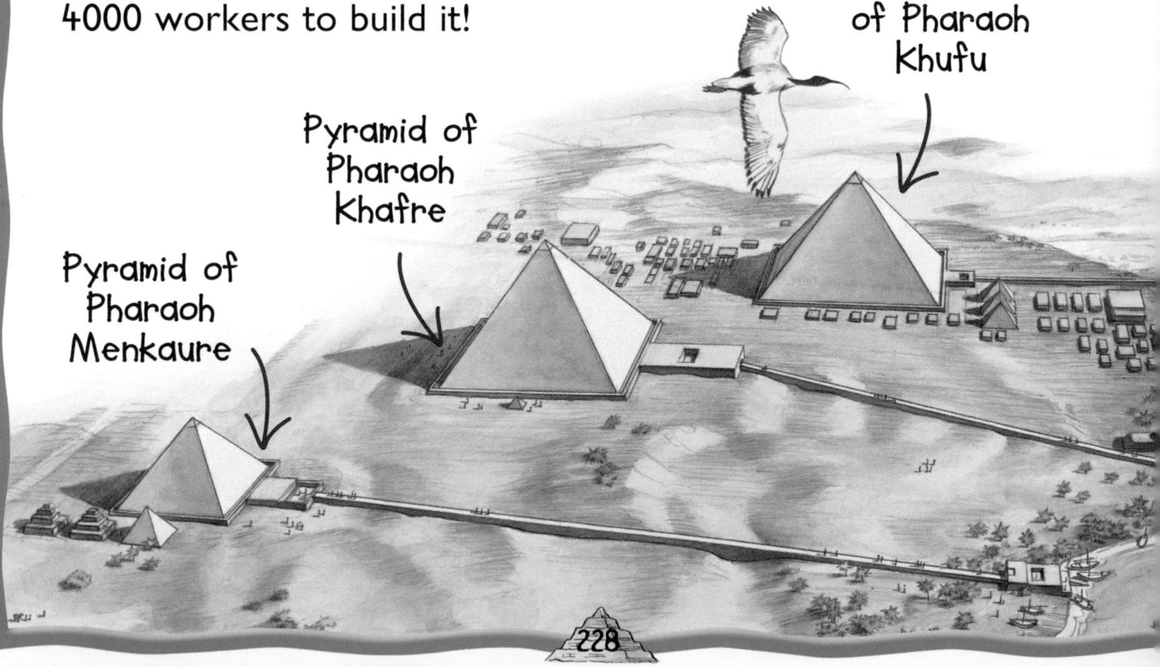

What guards the Great Pyramid?

The pyramids were full of treasures. A stone statue was built to guard the Great Pyramid at Giza. It was carved in the shape of a sphinx. A sphinx has the body of a lion and the head of a man. The sphinx at the Great Pyramid has the face of Pharaoh Khafre.

Tomb robbers!

'The Book of Buried Pearls' told robbers all about the treasures inside the tombs. It also showed them how to get past spirits that guarded the dead.

What was inside the Great Pyramid?

The Great Pyramid had two huge burial chambers. They were built for the pharaoh and his queen. A corridor called the Grand Gallery led to the pharaoh's chamber. The corridor's ceiling was 8 metres tall!

Map

Draw a plan of a pyramid. Include secret tunnels and hidden rooms to stop the robbers.

Who was the top god?

Ancient Egyptians worshipped more than 1000 gods. The most important was Ra, the Sun god. Every evening, Ra was swallowed by Nut, the sky goddess. At night, Ra travelled through the land of the dead. He was born again each morning. Later, Ra became Amun Ra, king of the gods.

Ra

Dead body god!

Anubis was the god in charge of dead bodies. He looked like a jackal, a kind of dog. People who wrapped bodies for burial often wore Anubis masks!

Why were cats important?

Cats were sacred (holy) animals in ancient Egypt. The goddess for cats, musicians and dancers was called Bastet. When a pet cat died it was wrapped up carefully and placed in a special cat-shaped coffin. Then the cat was buried in a cat cemetery!

Who took care of the temples?

Fabulous temples were built for the gods. Many temples were built for Amun Ra, king of the gods. Priests looked after the temples, their riches and the lands around them. These massive statues of Pharaoh Ramses II guard the temple at Abu Simbel.

Draw

Draw a picture of Ra travelling through the night in the land of the dead. He travelled in a boat.

How were the pyramids built?

Thousands of workers had to cut blocks of stone to the right shape using chisels and saws. Wooden sledges were then used to drag the stones to the pyramid. Each stone weighed more than two and a half big elephants!

Busy busy!

One ancient Egyptian was a very busy man! Imhotep was a doctor, a priest and a poet. He also designed and built a pyramid!

Were the pyramids painted white?

The finished pyramids had a bright white coating. This wasn't paint, but limestone, which protected the stones beneath. Inner walls were built from clay bricks that were lined with pink granite. White stone covered the floors.

How did the workers build so high?

The stones were pulled up a ramp to get to each level of the pyramid. The ramp was a steep slope made from baked earth bricks. The pyramid got higher and higher. So the ramp had to be made longer and longer! Sledges were pulled up the ramp on rollers.

Think

Look at the walls and ceilings of your house. What do you think they were built with?

How do you make a mummy?

Ancient Egyptians mummified their dead. First, the inside parts such as the brain, but not the heart, were removed. Then the body was salted and dried. Cloth was stuffed inside the body to help it keep its shape. Then the body was oiled and wrapped in lots of bandages.

Mummy case

All wrapped up!

The mummy was wrapped in tight bandages. This helped to stop the body from rotting away.

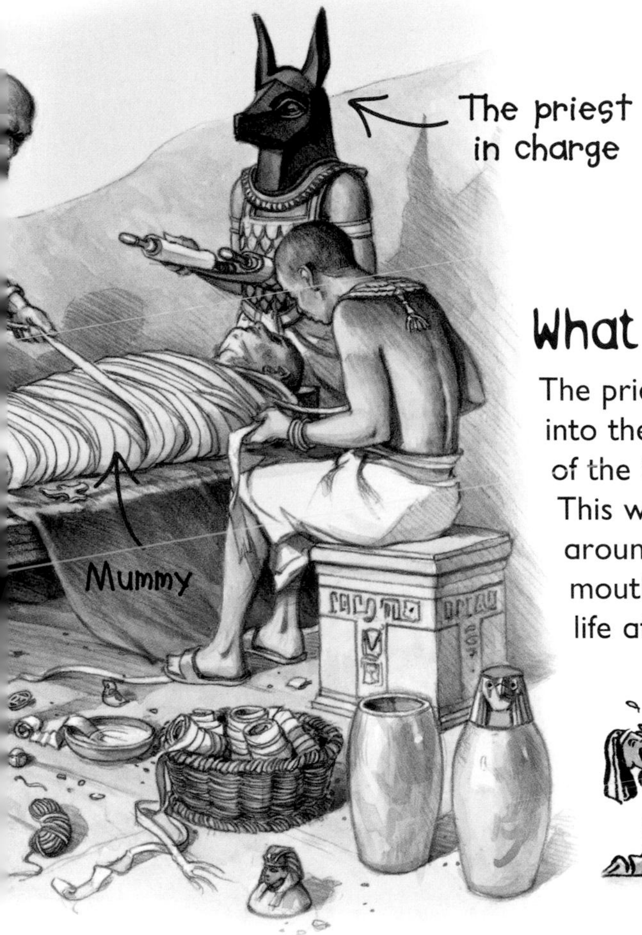

Make

Cut out a mummy mask from card and paint it with a face. It could be the face of an animal.

What did the priest do?

The priest sent the dead person's spirit into the next world. He touched parts of the body with special instruments. This was so that the body could move around in the world of the dead. The mouth could speak and eat in its new life after being touched!

What were mummies kept in?

The mummy was placed in a case. Some cases were just wooden boxes. Others were beautifully decorated. An important person, such as a pharaoh, was placed in a stone coffin called a sarcophagus (sarc-off-a-gus).

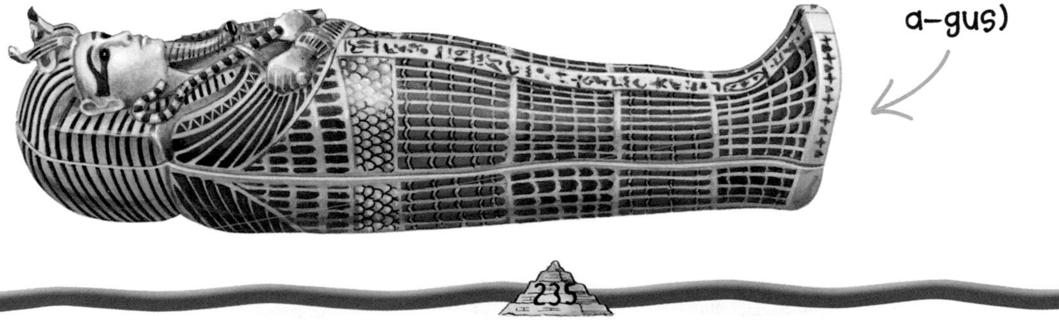

Did food grow in the desert?

Most of Egypt was in the hot desert. However, every year in July, the great river Nile flooded the dry fields. The water brought rich, black soil with it. This soil spread in wide strips on each side of the river. Farmers sowed their seed in this good soil.

How did the Egyptians farm?

Farmers used oxen and wooden ploughs to dig the soil. They weeded and dug channels with hoes. Then they planted seed, mostly by hand. Farmers also kept goats, sheep, ducks and geese. They kept bees to make honey.

Get lost!

Young boys were paid to be scarecrows! They frightened birds with their slingshots and loud shouts!

Farmers' crops

What did farmers grow?

Farmers grew barley for beer and grapes for wine. Dates, figs, melons, cucumbers, onions, leeks and lettuces grew well in the rich soil. Wheat was also grown to make bread.

Draw

Draw a basket full of crops grown by Egyptian farmers. You can see an Egyptian basket in this picture.

Who had the best jobs?

Doctors, high priests or priestesses and government officers had the best jobs.

So did viziers. A vizier helped the pharaoh to rule the land. Next came the traders and craftsmen, such as carpenters and jewellers. Labourers and farmhands had the poorest jobs.

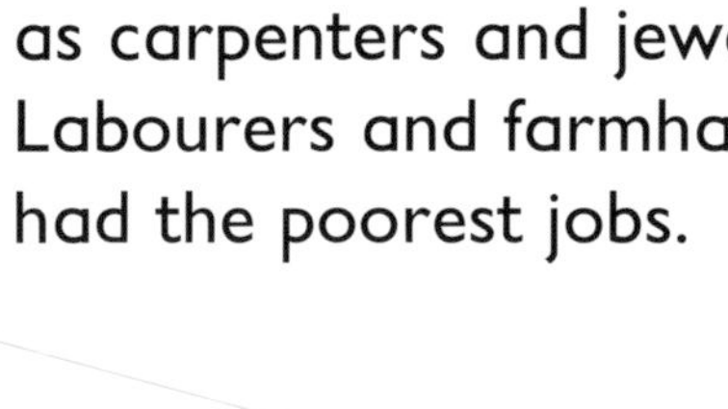

Who was head of the family?

In ancient Egypt the man was the head of the family. The eldest son was given all the land, property and riches when his father died. Women could also own land and property and get good jobs.

Little monkey!

Pet baboons were sometimes trained to climb fig trees and pick the ripe fruit!

Vizier checking grain

Imagine

Imagine you are an Egyptian worker. Which job would you choose to do and why?

What did children play with?

Children played with toys made from clay and wood. They had carved animals with legs and heads that could move. They also had spinning tops, clay balls, toy horses and dolls. Children played games such as leapfrog and tug-of-war, too.

Who had the biggest houses?

Rich Egyptians lived in large country houses called villas. Villas often had several storeys. Some had walled gardens with fruit orchards and a fish pond. Poor families often lived in one room. Many lived on crowded streets in the towns and cities.

How did the Egyptians cook?

Some ancient Egyptians cooked their food in a clay oven. Others cooked on an open fire. Clay ovens were made from baked clay bricks. Wood or charcoal were burned as fuel. Cooks used pottery saucepans with two handles.

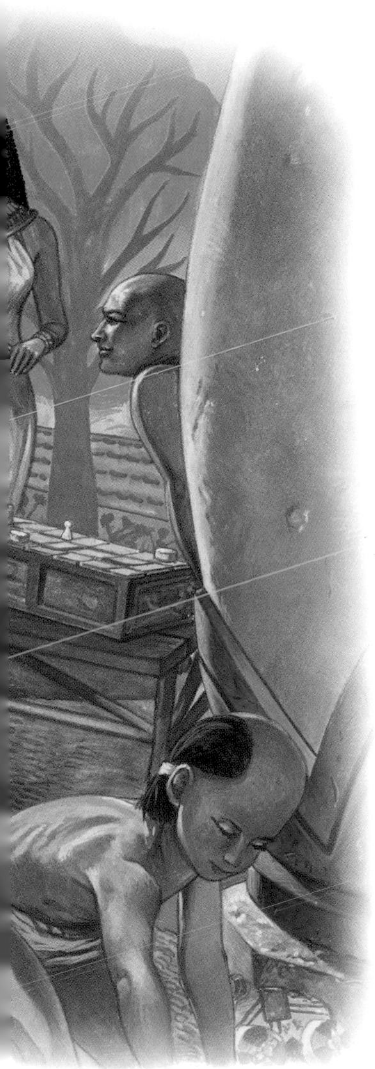

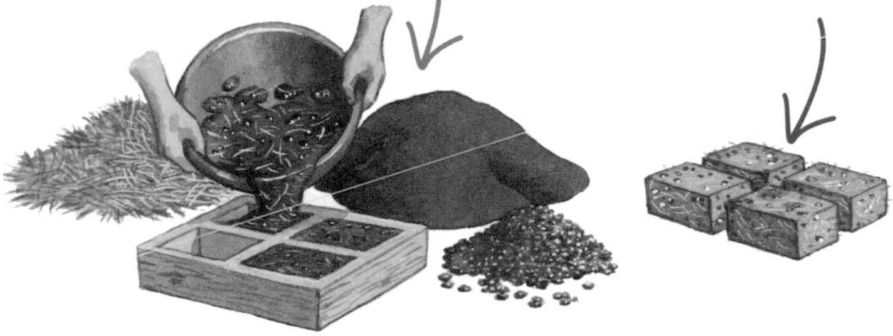

Were houses built with bricks?

Egyptian houses were built with bricks. Mud from the river Nile was mixed with straw and pebbles. The mixture was shaped into brick shapes and dried in the hot sun. Trunks from palm trees held up the flat roofs. Inside walls were plastered and painted.

Make

Mix clay with dried grass and pebbles. Put the mixture in an ice-cube tray. Let your bricks dry in the sun.

Sticky fingers!

Ancient Egyptians ate with their fingers. Rich people washed their hands between each dish. Their servants brought jugs of washing water for them.

Who shaved their hair off?

Both men and women shaved their hair off. They believed that this kept them clean. Men and women also wore make-up such as black kohl, which lined their eyes. Fingernail paint and face powder were also used. Red colouring was worn on lips and cheeks.

Cosy toes!

Rich people wore shoes made with padded leather. Sandals were made of the grass-like papyrus plant. Poor people went barefoot.

Did Egyptians ever wear wigs?

Rich Egyptians wore wigs made from human hair or sheep's wool. The wigs were kept in boxes held on stands. Egyptians also used hair dye. Girls plaited their hair into pigtails. Some boys wore a pigtail on one side.

Wigs

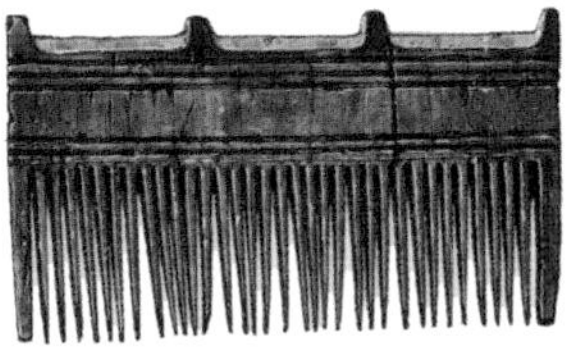

Wooden comb

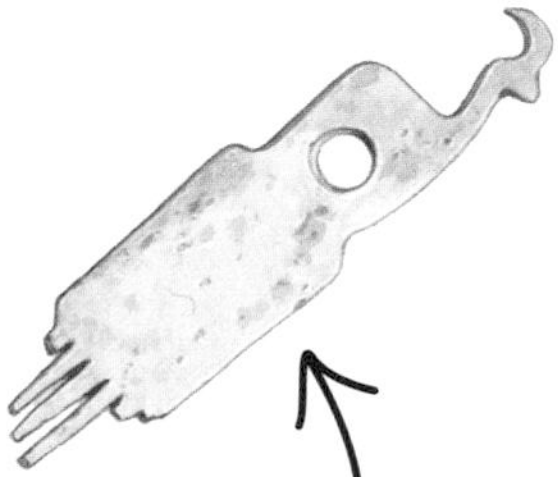

Ivory comb

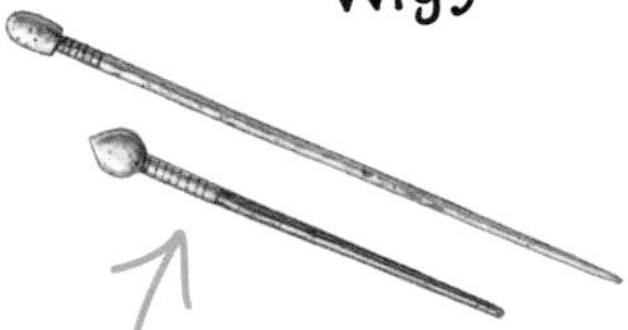

Hair pins

What was the fashion?

Rich women wore the best linen cloth with beads sewn onto it. The cloth was dyed in pale colours. It was made into long dresses and cloaks. Men wore long robes. They also wore cloths wrapped around the waist. These were tied in a knot.

Make

Draw an Egyptian wearing clothes and make-up. Use wool to make a wig. Glue this to the person's head.

Who were the workers?

Most Egyptians were labourers who worked on farms and building sites. There were also carpenters, potters, jewellers and shoemakers. These people were called craftworkers and they had shops in towns. Some worked for rich people.

Craftworker

Draw

Draw symbols for different jobs. Try a hammer for a carpenter or a ring for a jeweller.

How did Egyptians write?

Egyptians used symbols for writing. These were called hieroglyphs. Some hieroglyphs stood for words. Others stood for sounds. School children had to learn 700 different hieroglyphs!

School children

Did people write on paper?

The Egyptians had no paper. Instead they wrote on papyrus. This was made from reeds that grew next to the river Nile. Papyrus lasts a long time. Sheets of it have survived 3000 years!

Packed lunch!

Workers took bread, onions and a cucumber for their lunch. They washed it down with weak beer.

Quiz time

Do you remember what you have read about Egypt?

These questions will test your memory. The pictures will help you. If you get stuck, read the pages again.

page 229

1. What guards the Great Pyramid?

page 231

2. Why were cats important?

3. What were mummies kept in?

page 235

4. What did the priest do?

page 235

5. What did farmers grow?

page 237

6. Who was head of the family?

page 238

7. What did children play with?

page 239

8. How did the Egyptians cook?

page 240

9. Who shaved their hair off?

page 242

10. What was the fashion?

page 243

11. Did Egyptians ever wear wigs?

page 243

12. Did people write on paper?

page 245

13. How did Egyptians write?

page 245

Answers

1. The sphinx
2. Because they were holy
3. Mummy case or sarcophagus
4. Sent the dead person's spirit into the next world
5. Barley, grapes, dates, figs, melons, cucumbers, onions, leeks and lettuces
6. The man
7. Wooden or clay toys, spinning tops, clay balls, toy horses and dolls
8. With clay ovens or open fires
9. Men and women
10. Dresses, cloaks and long robes
11. Rich Egyptians did
12. No, they wrote on papyrus
13. Egyptians used symbols to write

Questions about...

Ancient Rome

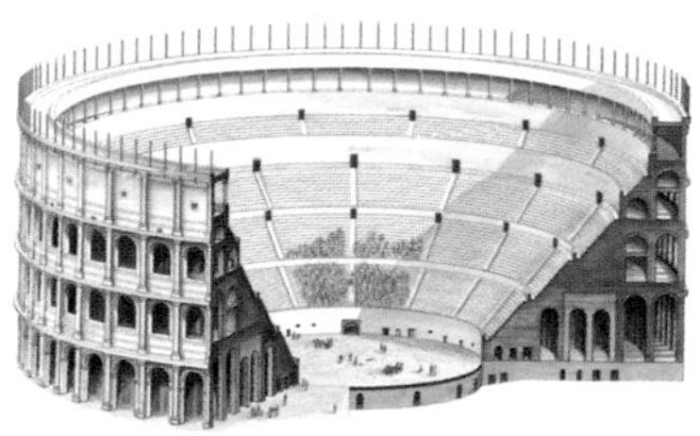

What was the Roman Empire?

Rome is a city in modern-day Italy. About 3000 years ago, it was just a small village. It began to grow into a large, powerful city. About 2000 years ago, Rome ruled many different lands. All of these lands, including Rome itself, were known as the Roman Empire.

Find out

The Roman Empire was huge. Try to find out which countries were part of it.

Where did people go shopping?

Rome had the world's first shopping centre. It was called Trajan's Market, and was built on five different levels on the slopes of a hill in the centre of Rome. It contained more than 150 shops in a large main hall.

Time to go!

The Romans designed the first public toilets. Users sat next to each other on rows of seats.

Did people live in blocks of flats?

The Romans built the world's first high-rise flats. Most people who lived in Ostia, a busy town close to Rome, lived in blocks of flats known as 'insulae'. Each block had up to 100 small rooms.

Blocks of flats

What did the Romans eat?

People ate just bread and fruit for breakfast. Lunch might be leftovers from the night before. The main meal was eaten in the evening. It might include meat such as goose or hare, and vegetables and fruit. It took all day to prepare.

Preparing dinner

Plan

Find out what the Romans ate then plan your own Roman menu. Include a starter, main dish and dessert.

Did people have dinner parties?

Yes, they did – and they lay down to eat! People lay on long couches around a table. They often wore crowns of flowers and they took off their sandals before entering the dining room.

Dinner party

Yuk!

Yummy dishes for a Roman banquet might include eel, thrush, dormouse or poached snails. If that upset people's stomachs, pickled cabbage was eaten to make them feel better!

Who ate takeaways?

Ordinary people did. Many went to cheap eating houses for their main meal, or bought ready-cooked snacks from roadside fast-food stalls.

What did children learn at school?

Only boys went to school. At the age of six they began to learn reading, writing, arithmetic, history and sport. They were also taught public speaking.

At school

Inky fingers!

Soot from wood fires was used to make ink. It was mixed with vinegar and sticky gum that oozed from trees. Some Roman writing has survived 2000 years.

Did children use calculators?

Calculators hadn't been invented, so children learned to count with their fingers! A wooden counting frame called an abacus was used to work out sums.

Count

If boys started school aged 6 and left when they were 16, how many years did they study for?

Why didn't girls go to school?

Roman girls were expected to stay at home and learn how to run a household. This was training for when they were married. Most girls were taught how to play a musical instrument called the lyre.

Learning to play the lyre

What was a toga?

Most men wore a long robe called a toga. It looked good, but it was bulky and uncomfortable to wear. Important men wore togas with a purple trim. Most children wore togas, too. Married ladies wore a dress called a 'stola' and a shawl called a 'palla' over the top of it.

Did people wear make-up?

Both men and women wore make-up. The Romans admired pale, smooth skin. Crushed chalk was used as face powder, red ochre (crumbly earth) for blusher and plant juice for lipstick.

'Scare' cut!

Going to the barbers could be very painful. Scissors and razors had not been invented. Barbers used big, sharp shears to trim men's hair and beards!

Find out

What did Julius Caesar wear on his head?

What were Roman hairstyles like?

Hairstyles went in and out of fashion. Women would curl, plait or pin up their hair. Wigs and hair extensions were popular, as were headdresses and hairbands.

Who wore precious jewels?

Men and women wore rings of gold, silver or bronze. Many of these rings were decorated with amber or precious stones. Rich ladies wore necklaces and earrings of gold and pearls, while poorer women made do with beads of glass or ceramics. Cloaks were fastened with fine brooches.

Baby love!

Romans gave a good luck charm called a 'bulla' to their babies to keep them safe from harm.

What was a mosaic?

The Romans liked their homes to look good, too. Beautiful pictures called mosaics decorated floors. Each mosaic was made from thousands of small tiles made from coloured stone or pottery.

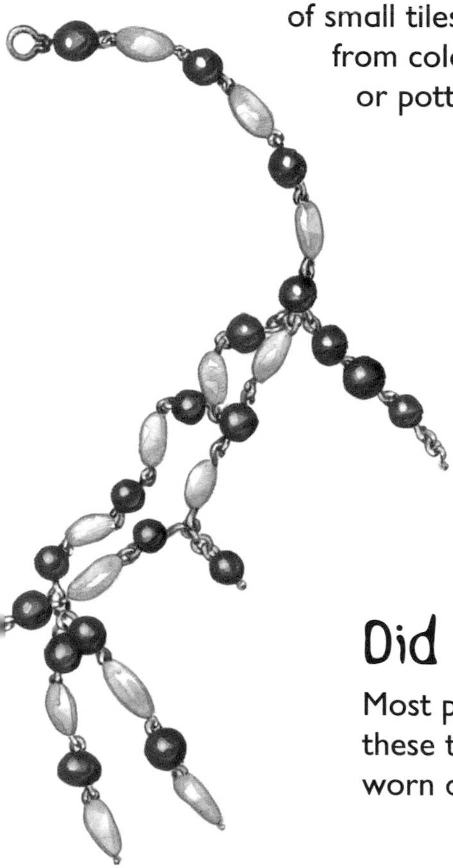

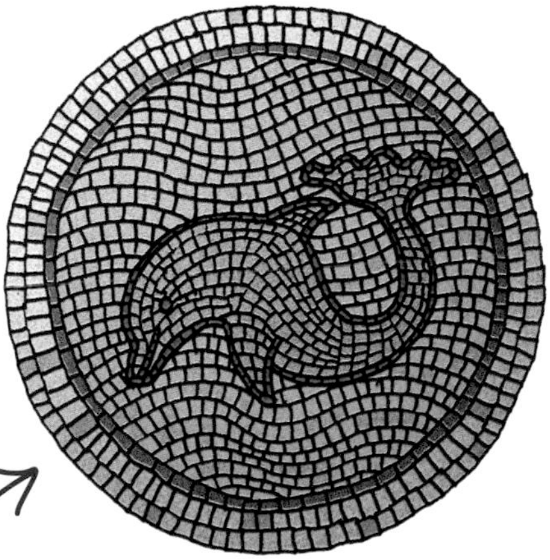

Mosaic

Make

Look at some Roman mosaics in a book then make your own using squares of coloured card.

Did people wear shoes?

Most people wore leather sandals. Soldiers wore these too, but with studded soles so they were not worn out by marching. Boots were worn for riding.

How clean were the Romans?

The Romans were sometimes very clean. They visited public baths. These huge buildings were also fitness centres and a place to meet friends. Visitors could take part in sports, such as wrestling, have a massage or even get their hair cut.

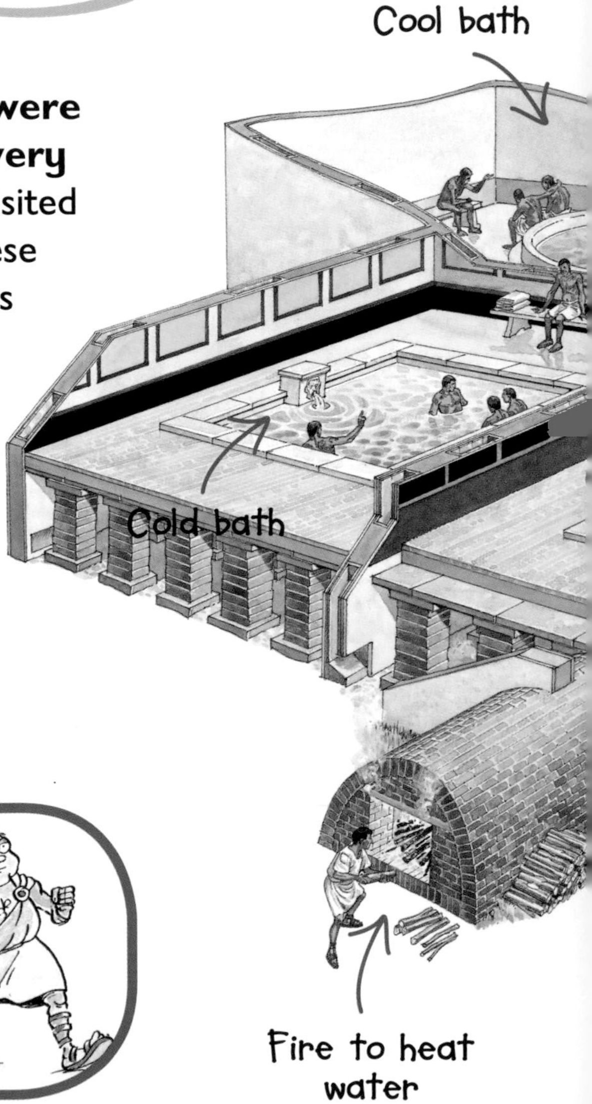

What a stink!

Although the Romans liked bathing, they only visited the baths once in every nine days.

Did the Romans listen to music?

The Romans liked music and dancing. Ordinary people liked listening to pipes, flutes, cymbals and horns. Rich people preferred the quieter sound of the lyre.

Think

Roman baths were a good place for people to meet their friends. Think about where you go to meet your friends.

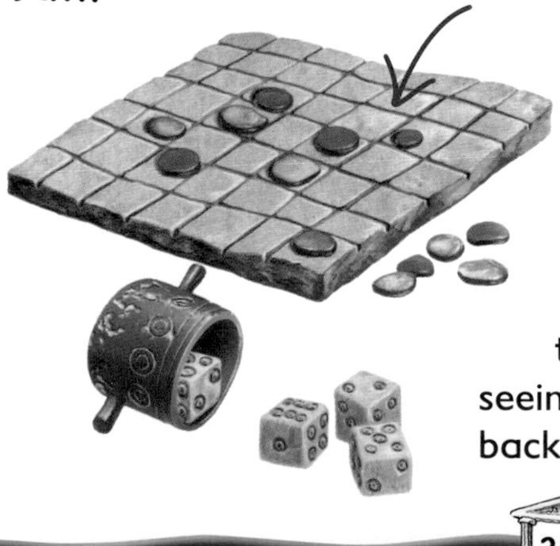

What games did people play?

Popular Roman games were 'Tables', 'Robbers' and 'Three Stones' – a version of noughts-and-crosses. A favourite girls' game was tossing little bones into the air and seeing how many they could catch on the back of the hand.

What was the Colosseum?

The Colosseum was an amazing building. It was a huge oval arena in the centre of Rome, used for fights between men called gladiators, and for pretend sea battles. Up to 50,000 people could sit inside. It was built of stone, concrete and marble and had 80 entrances.

Draw

Romans followed chariot racing like we support football. Draw a poster advertising a chariot race.

Did Romans race to the circus?

The Romans liked a day at the races. Horses pulled chariots around a track, called a 'circus'. The most famous was Circus Maximus. Twelve chariots took part in each race, running seven times round the track.

Chariot racing

Superstars!

Some gladiators became so popular that people wrote graffiti about them on walls.

Was chariot racing dangerous?

Yes it was. Chariots often smashed into each other and overturned. Each driver carried a sharp knife called a 'falx', to cut himself free if this happened. Many horses and drivers were killed.

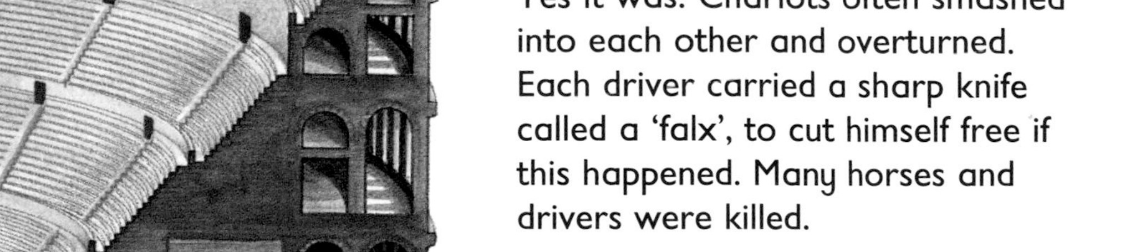

What was army life like?

Roman soldiers were well paid and well cared for. They were often called upon to defend the Roman Empire from enemies, so the army was very important. Soldiers were trained in battle and often had to march long distances along straight roads.

Brrrr!

Roman soldiers guarding the cold northern frontiers of Britain kept warm by wearing short woollen trousers, like underpants, beneath their tunics!

Testudo

Did soldiers cook dinner?

Yes they did. Soldiers had to find or make everything they needed to survive. They built camps and forts defended by walls. Soldiers had to be able to cook, build, and be doctors, blacksmiths and engineers – and they all had to fight!

Was a tortoise used in battle?

When soldiers had to defend themselves against enemy attack, they used a 'tortoise'. Their shields made a protective 'shell' around them. It was called a 'testudo', or tortoise. Soldiers carried three main weapons – javelins, swords and daggers.

Roman soldiers

Discover

Can you find out which famous British queen the Romans had trouble defeating?

What was a villa?

Villas were large Roman country houses. They were surrounded by orchards, fields, flocks of sheep or herds of cattle. Country villas were owned mainly by the rich. The first villas were small farmhouses, but as Rome became powerful, villas became magnificent mansions.

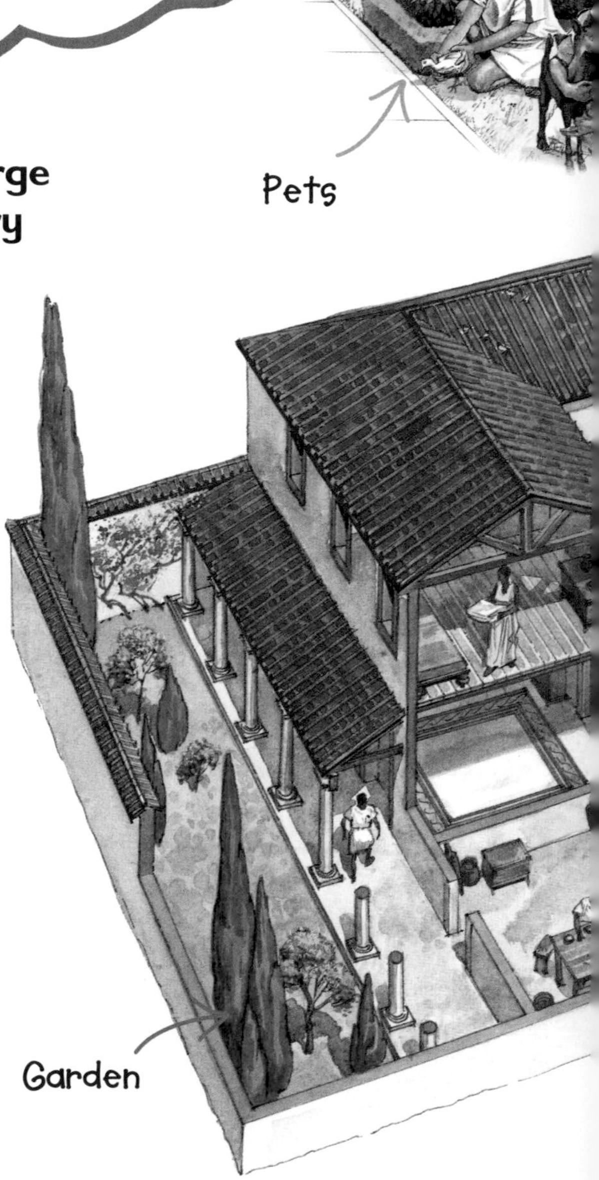

Plan

Plan your own villa. Draw pictures of how it might look.

Did people keep pets?

Roman families liked to keep pets. Statues and paintings show many children playing with their pets. Dogs, cats and doves were all popular. Some families also kept ornamental fish and tame deer.

Love struck!

The Romans invented Valentine's Day, but called it 'Lupercalia'. Boys picked a girl's name from a hat, and she was meant to be their girlfriend for the year!

Where did people go on holiday?

In the summer, Rome became hot, stuffy, smelly and dirty. Rich Romans often had two homes, so they would leave the city and escape to their villa in the countryside.

Why were farms important?

In Roman times, most people lived and worked on farms. Without farms, the people of Rome would starve. Farmers produced food for city people, which was grown on big estates by teams of slaves, and on small peasant farms where single families worked together.

Squeaky clean!

When Romans bathed, they covered their bodies in olive oil and then scraped it off to remove all the dirt and sweat!

Why were olives so special?

Olives grow on trees. The Romans used them as food, or crushed them to make oil. Olive oil was used as medicine, in cooking, for cleansing the skin – and even for burning in lamps.

Imagine

Imagine you are a Roman farm worker, what job would you do and why?

Did grapes grow on trees?

Roman grapes did grow on trees, almost! Vines are climbing plants that produce grapes. The Romans planted them among fruit trees, which supported the vines as they grew.

Who was the top god?

The Romans worshipped many different gods. Jupiter was king of the gods. His wife Juno was worshipped by married women. Mars was the god of war and Venus was the goddess of love. Neptune, god of the sea, sent earthquakes and terrible storms. Messenger of the gods was Mercury.

Jupiter and Juno

Mars and Venus

Neptune

Find out

School children had their own goddess. Can you find out what she was called? Use a book to help you.

Did people go to church?

Temples were beautiful buildings. They were built so that people could worship the gods. At the centre was a shrine. Here, people would leave food and wine as gifts to the gods.

Animal magic!

The Romans believed they could foretell the future by watching animals. For example, bees were a sign of riches but a hooting owl meant danger!

Temple

Which god started storms?

Neptune was god of the sea. The Romans believed he could start and stop storms. He was also the god of earthquakes. Sea travel was dangerous in Roman times, so sailors prayed to Neptune to keep them safe on their journeys.

Mercury

Why were roads always straight?

The Romans built thousands of kilometres of roads. They were built to link the rest of the empire to Rome itself. To make travel as fast as possible, roads were built in straight lines taking the shortest route.

Look

The Romans invented concrete. Look outside – can you see anything made of concrete?

Could ships sail to Rome?

Most ships were too big to sail up the river Tiber to Rome. Instead, they stopped at Rome's main port, Ostia. Here, the ship's cargo was loaded onto smaller barges and taken the final 25 kilometres to Rome.

Roman ship

Crystal ball!

The Romans often consulted a fortune-teller or a priest even before setting out on a long journey.

Did people travel in their beds?

Town streets were crowded and very dirty. Rich people travelled in curtained beds called litters, carried shoulder-high by slaves. Ordinary people used stepping-stones to avoid the mud and rubbish on the streets.

Why was Rome so beautiful?

The Romans built beautiful buildings. They invented concrete, and used clay bricks baked at high temperatures, which lasted longer than unbaked ones. Arches were built to create strong walls and doorways. Huge domes were made for buildings that were too big for wooden roofs.

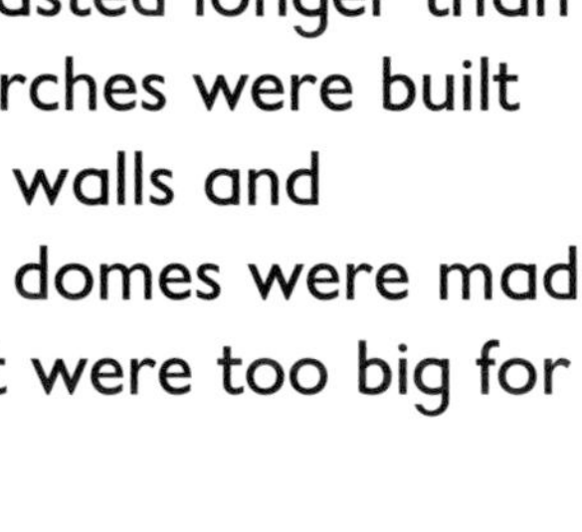

Pipe up!

Our word 'plumber' comes from 'plumbum', the Latin word for the lead used by Romans to make water pipes. The same word is also used for a 'plumb-line', still in use today.

Roman buildings

Were there doctors in Rome?

Yes there were, but the Romans believed that illness was caused by witchcraft. To find a cure, they visited a temple to ask the gods to make them better. They might see a doctor who made medicines from plants or carried out simple operations.

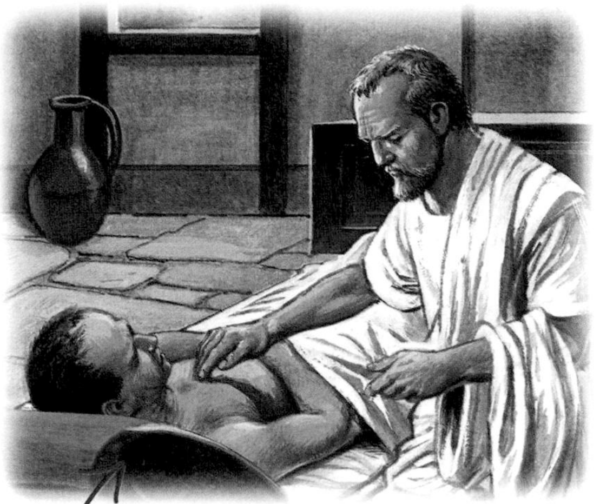

Doctor and patient

Find out

Romans spoke their own language. Can you find out what it was called?

How was Rome supplied with water?

Water from mountain springs was carried on raised stone channels into the city. Once the water reached the city, it flowed through pipes to baths, fountains and toilets.

Quiz time

Do you remember what you have read about ancient Rome? Here are some questions to test your memory. The pictures will help you. If you get stuck, read the pages again.

page 251

1. Did people live in blocks of flats?

page 253

2. Who ate takeaways?

3. What did children learn at school?

page 254

4. What was a mosaic?

page 259

page 260

5. How clean were the Romans?

6. Did the Romans listen to music?

page 261

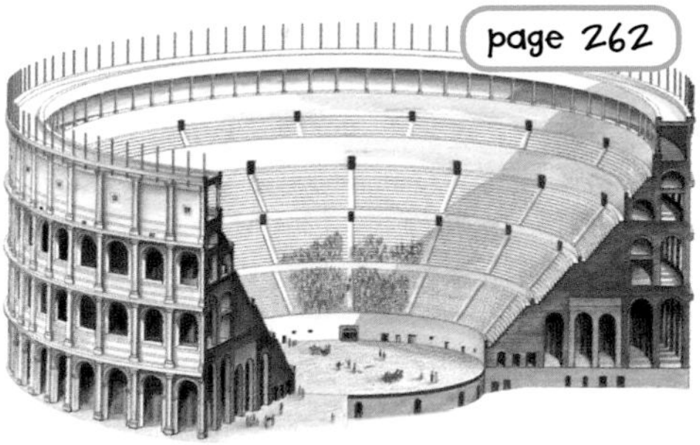

page 262

7. What was the Colosseum?

8. Did people keep pets?

page 267

page 269

9. Why were olives so special?

10. Did grapes grow on trees?

page 269

11. Who was the top god?

page 270

12. Did people travel in their beds?

page 273

13. Why was Rome so beautiful?

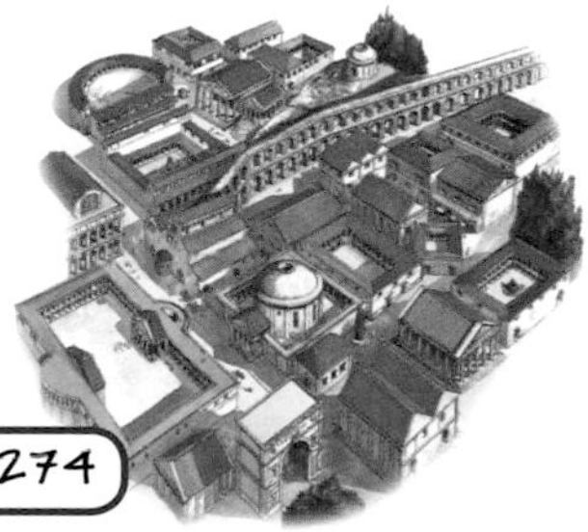

page 274

Answers

1. Yes, Rome had the first high-rise flats
2. Poorer people
3. Writing, arithmetic, history, sport, public speaking
4. Pictures made from coloured stone or pottery
5. Very clean, when they visited the baths
6. Yes, they liked music and dancing
7. A huge oval arena used for gladiator fights and pretend sea battles
8. Yes they did
9. Because they were used as food and crushed to make oil that was used for many things
10. Grapes grew on vines that grew around trees
11. Jupiter
12. No, they travelled in litters
13. Because the Romans built beautiful buildings

Questions about...

Vikings

Where did Vikings come from?

The Vikings lived about 2000 years ago. Viking warriors came from Denmark, Sweden and Norway to raid villages and steal treasure. Viking families began to settle in England, Ireland, Scotland and France. They explored Iceland, Greenland and Russia – and even travelled as far as North America.

Who discovered Greenland?

A Viking called Erik the Red discovered Greenland. It was a dark and icy place but Erik wanted people to come and live there. He called it 'Greenland' so they would think it was a warm place full of trees and grass.

Greenland

Imagine

Can you imagine discovering a new country? What would you call it?

Why did Vikings carry their boats?

In winter, Vikings made long overland journeys. In some places, they carried their boats over ground between rivers. The Vikings were brave adventurers, keen to seek new land and treasures. Each journey took several years.

Pirates!

The word 'Viking' means 'pirates', 'port-attackers', or 'people of the bays'. This tells us that Vikings spent their lives close to the sea.

Which king killed his brother?

When a Viking king died, each of his sons had an equal right to his throne. Erik Bloodaxe was famous for his cruelty. He wanted to be king so much, he killed both of his brothers and became King Erik of Norway.

Think

What would your Viking name be? You can make it as funny as you like!

My name is...!

Many Viking rulers had strange names such as Svein Forkbeard, Einar Falsemouth, Magnus Barelegs, and Thorfinn Skullsplitter!

Who tried to stop the waves?

King Cnut was a Viking king of Denmark, Norway and England. He was a cruel ruler. However, Cnut said he was a good Christian. To prove it, he ordered the waves to stop. When they did not he said, "This proves that I am weak. Only God can control the sea."

What was the Jelling Stone?

King Harald Bluetooth built a church at Jelling, in Denmark. Outside the church was a memorial for his dead parents. It was called the Jelling Stone and was decorated with Viking and Christian carvings.

What was a dragon ship?

Vikings built ships called 'drakar', or dragon ships. These ships were designed for war. They were long, speedy and beautifully carved. Because they were so light, they could sail easily onto beaches.

Drakar ship

Did Vikings have maps?

No, they didn't. The Vikings used the positions of the Sun, Moon and stars to guide them on their travels. They also followed the direction the wind was blowing in.

Remember

Can you remember the Viking word for 'dragon ship'?

Gold to go away!

Viking pirates threatened to attack if they were not paid to sail away. This usually worked, and villages paid the gold – again and again!

Who was afraid of the Vikings?

Vikings could be very scary! People living in seaside villages were often afraid of them. Gangs of warriors carried out raids on defenceless villages. They stole valuable treasure and healthy young men and women to sell as slaves.

Viking raid

Why were Vikings so fierce?

To scare their enemies in battle! Viking warriors dressed in animal skins and charged at their enemies, howling and growling like wolves, and chewing at their shields. These warriors were called berserkirs and this is where the word 'berserk' comes from.

Berserkir

Did swords have names?

Viking warriors loved their swords so much, they even gave them names such as 'Sharp Biter'! When a warrior died, he would be buried with his sword by his side.

Design

Draw your own Viking sword and shield. What name would you give to your sword?

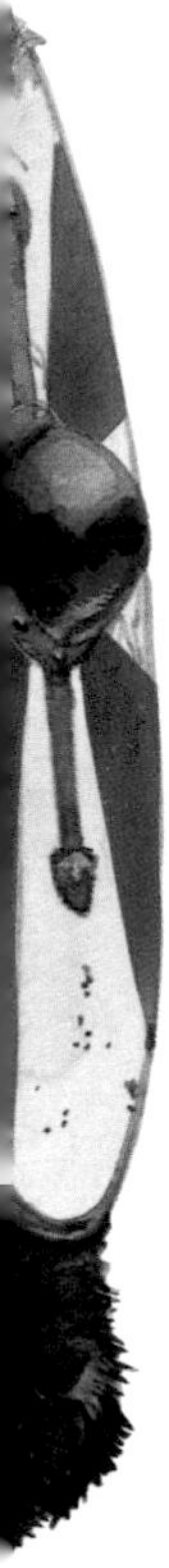

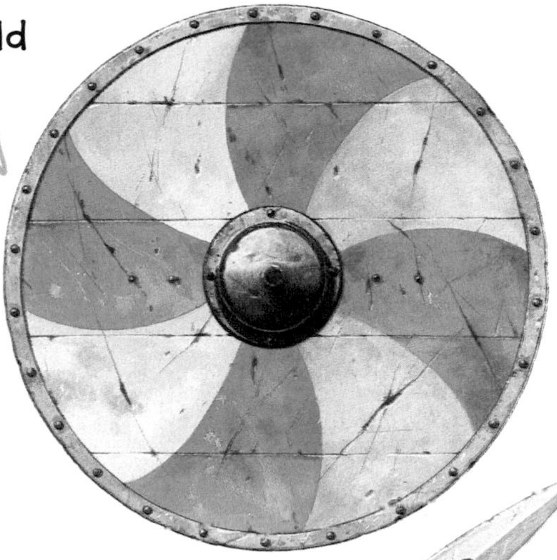

What weapons did Vikings use?

Vikings had to make or buy all of their weapons. Poor soldiers carried knives and spears. Wealthy Vikings had metal helmets and tunics, and fine, sharp swords. They carried a round shield that was made of wood covered with leather.

Soldier women!

Women went to war but they did not fight. Instead, they nursed wounded warriors and cooked meals for hungry soldiers.

Who rode an eight-legged horse?

Odin was king of the Viking gods. He rode an eight-legged horse called Sleipnir and had two ravens called Thought and Memory. Odin sat on a high throne so he could see all of the Universe. Sometimes he liked to dress as a traveller and take a holiday in the human world.

Discover

Can you find out about any other Viking gods or goddesses – which one is your favourite?

Who controlled the thunder?

The storm god Thor controlled thunder. Viking farmers hated thunderstorms because they ruined their crops. They would pray to Thor to stop the thunder and let their crops grow. Thor rode in his chariot through the clouds holding a giant hammer and thunderbolt.

Sea god!

Njord was the god of the sea. He was married to the giantess Skadi, who watched over the mountains.

Why were warriors so brave?

Because they believed they would go to heaven when they died. Vikings thought that dead warriors were remembered forever, and that they went to heaven to feast with the gods.

Why did animals live in houses?

Homes were needed to shelter animals, as well as people. In towns, pigs, goats and horses were kept in sheds. In the countryside, the weather could be cold and wet. Farmers lived in longhouses, with an area for animals at one end. This meant that the people and animals stayed warm and dry.

What were runes?

Runes were the 16 letters of the Viking alphabet. People used them for labelling belongings with the owner's name, recording accounts, keeping calendars and sending messages. There was no paper, so runes were carved onto wood.

Runes

Make

With a cardboard box, make your own Viking house. You could even glue some grass to the roof.

Why did Vikings get ill?

Vikings suffered from chest diseases. This was because their houses did not have windows and were often damp and full of smoke from the fire burning on the stove.

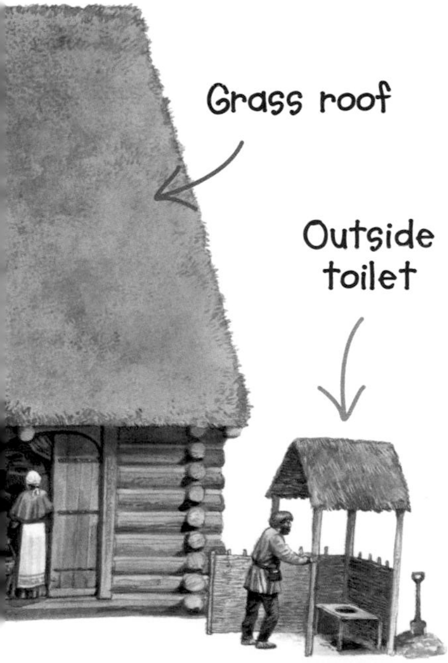

Precious cow!

Viking farmers loved cows! A cow was precious because it gave milk, clothing and meat, and its droppings were spread on the fields to help crops grow.

How did grass provide food?

Grassy fields provided food for animals and people. Sheep and cows needed fresh grass to eat. These animals then provided milk and meat for people to eat. Farmers also cut the grass and dried it out to make hay to feed the animals in the winter.

Have a look at the labels inside your clothes. What are your clothes made of?

Did Vikings have factories?

No! Vikings had no machines, so all work was done by hand. Families had to make or grow everything they needed. They built their own houses and furniture and they made their own clothes and toys. Blacksmiths made weapons and tools for people to work with.

Why was the sea so important?

Because people could catch fish to eat. People also gathered shellfish from the seashore for dinner. Vikings built their villages close to the sea in case they needed to travel to new places.

Itchy clothes!

Clothes were made of wool and could be very itchy. Women made smoother, finer cloth to wear as underwear.

What was sold at markets?

Vikings held markets on the beach. Farmers would sell meat, milk and fur to travellers. Some Vikings travelled a long way to buy different things to sell. They would buy woollen cloth from Britain, wine from France, glass from Germany, jewellery from Russia and spices from the Middle East.

How were quarrels settled?

Many quarrels were settled by fighting. Quarrels between families could continue for months. This lead to people on both sides being killed, until each family was prepared to seek peace.

Settling an argument

Bone comb!

Animal bones that were left over from mealtimes were used to carve combs, beads and pins. Deer antlers were used to make finer combs.

Pretend

With a friend, pretend to be a pirate and Viking. Who is more scared of who?

Who were the Vikings scared of?

Pirates from Russia! They sailed across the sea to steal treasure from Viking towns. So Vikings defended their towns with wooden walls and troops of warriors.

Did girls go to school?

No, they didn't. Instead of going to school, girls helped their mothers with cooking and cleaning, fed farm animals, fetched water, gathered wood, nuts and berries and learned how to spin, weave and sew.

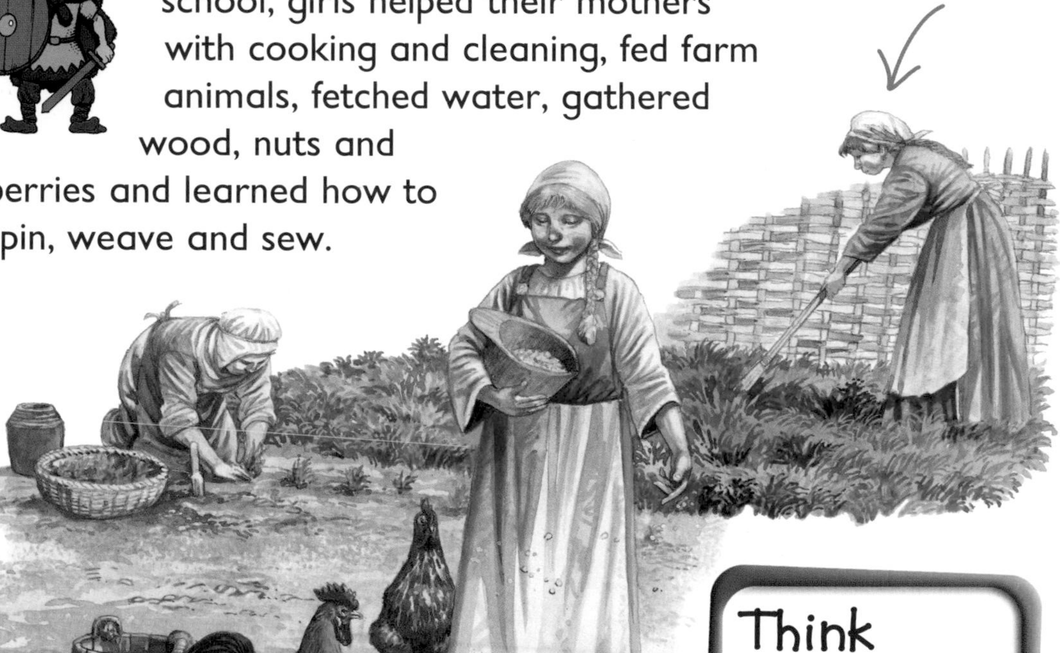

Think

Can you think why it was important for young boys to practise fighting with wooden swords?

Were wives expensive?

If a Viking man wanted to marry, he had to ask the woman's father for permission and pay him a bride price. If the father accepted this, the marriage went ahead, even if the woman did not agree.

Who used wooden swords?

Viking boys practised fighting with wooden swords and small, lightweight shields. They also learned how to ride horses and use real weapons. They had to be ready to fight by the time they were 15 or 16 years old.

Viking boys

Wise women!

Many young women died having a baby. This meant there were fewer older women. Older women were thought to be very wise and people respected them for their knowledge and experience.

What did people wear?

Vikings wore lots of layers to keep out the cold. Women wore long dresses of linen or wool with a woollen over-dress. Men dressed in wool tunics over linen shirts and woollen trousers. Men also wore fur or sheepskin caps while women wore headscarves and shawls.

Dress up

Have a look through your wardrobe and see if you can dress up as a Viking!

Glass jewels!

The Vikings imported broken glass from Germany, to melt and recycle into beautiful glass beads.

Did people wear jewellery?

Both men and women liked to wear lots of jewellery. They thought it made them look good and it also showed how rich they were. Rings and arm braclets were given to warriors as rewards for fighting bravely in battle.

Gold ring

Necklace

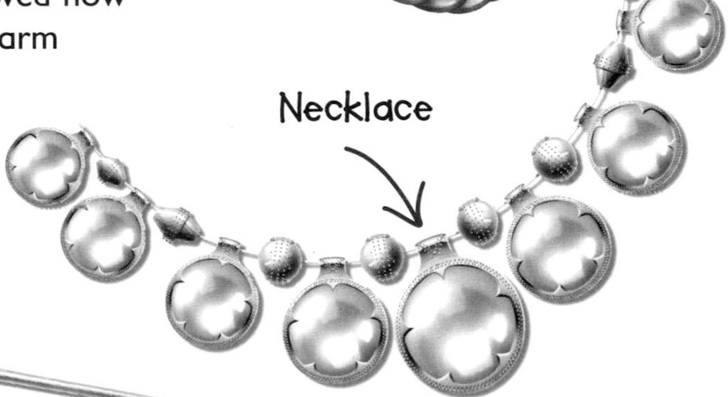

Brooch

Did Vikings wear make up?

Viking men wore make-up! They particularly liked to wear make up around their eyes – probably made from soot or crushed berries. They thought it made them look more handsome.

How did people get clean?

Vikings bathed by pouring water over red-hot stones to create clouds of steam. They sat in the steam to make themselves sweat, then rubbed their skin with birch twigs to help loosen the dirt. Then they jumped into a pool of cold water to rinse off.

Keeping clean

Did Vikings have toilets?

Yes they did. Houses had an outside toilet that was simply a bucket, or a hole in the ground with a wooden seat on top. Panels of woven twigs were set up around the toilet. Dried moss or grass was used as toilet paper.

Sloping house!

Longhouses were built on a slope. Then waste from the animals ran downhill – away from people living inside!

Hairstyles

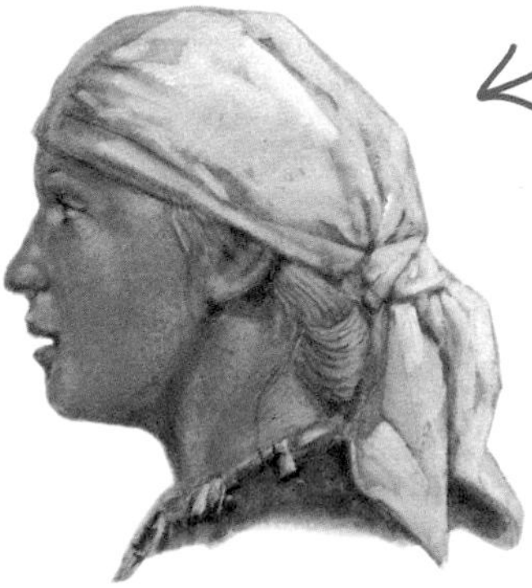

How did Vikings wear their hair?

Men let their fringes grow long, and plaited the strands that hung down either side of their face. Women also kept their hair long. They left it flowing loose until they married, then tied it in a beautiful knot at the nape of their neck.

Try

Is your hair long enough to plait like a Viking? Ask an adult to help you.

How did Vikings prepare for battle?

Viking sports were good training for war. Spear-throwing, sword-fighting and archery – shooting at targets with bows and arrows – were all popular. They helped boys and young men to become fit and strong and prepared them for using weapons.

Archer

Drinking horns

Vikings liked to drink ale from cups carved from cattle horns. Warriors would carry these drinking horns on their long journeys.

What was a saga?

A saga was a story that Vikings told to honour heroes who died in battle. The sagas were told to ensure that heroes' names and fame never died. These stories were passed on by word of mouth for many years.

Saga

What did people do for fun?

Vikings liked music and dancing. Kings would hire dancers, clowns, jugglers and singers to entertain their guests at feasts. Vikings also enjoyed playing practical jokes and listening to stories about gods and heroes.

Write

What is your favourite story? Maybe you could try and write one of your own.

Who defeated the Vikings?

Kings of England, Scotland and Wales defeated the Vikings. In 1014, King Brian Boru drove the Vikings from Ireland, and Viking rule ended in England in 1042. Viking kings still ruled parts of Scotland until 1266.

Viking defeat

Find out

Try to find any other Viking words that we still use today. Ask an adult to help you.

Festival

How do we remember the Vikings?

Today, people still celebrate Viking festivals. In the Shetland Isles, people dress up as Vikings then burn a lifesize model of a Viking warship. They do this to remember the Viking festival of Yule, held every January.

Do you speak Viking?

Many Viking words for everyday things still survive such as 'sister', 'knife' and 'egg'.

Was Santa a Viking?

Santa was a Viking god! Yule (mid-winter) was an important Viking festival. Vikings held feasts and exchanged gifts. They also believed that Viking gods travelled across the sky, bringing good things – just like Santa!

Quiz time

Do you remember what you have read about the Vikings? These questions will test your memory. The pictures will help you. If you get stuck, read the pages again.

page 281

1. Why did Vikings carry their boats?

2. Which king killed his brother?

page 282

3. Who was afraid of the Vikings?

page 285

4. Did swords have names?

page 286

5. Who controlled the thunder?

page 289

6. Why did animals live in houses?

page 290

7. Why was the sea so important?

page 293

page 300

11. Did Vikings have toilets?

8. Who used wooden swords?

page 297

12. Who defeated the Vikings?

page 304

9. Were wives expensive?

page 297

page 305

13. Was Santa a Viking?

10. How did people get clean?

page 300

Answers

1. To transport them between rivers
2. Erik Bloodaxe
3. People living in seaside villages
4. Viking warriors gave their swords names
5. Thor, the storm god
6. To keep them warm and dry
7. So people could catch fish to eat
8. Viking boys
9. Viking men had to pay money to their bride's father
10. They steamed themselves
11. Yes, they did
12. Kings of England, Scotland and Wales
13. Yes, Santa was a Viking god

Questions about...

Knights & Castles

Why were castles built on hills?

People began building castles over 1000 years ago. They were built on a hill so that people could see the enemy better. The hill was made from a huge mound of mud and stones. It was called a motte.

Were all castles made from wood?

Early castles were made from wood. They were not very strong and they caught fire easily. People began to build stone castles. These were much stronger. They lasted longer and did not burn.

Stone castle

Slimy walls!

Builders often covered wooden castles with wet, slippery leather. This stopped them from burning so easily.

What was a moat?

Builders dug a big ditch around the castle. Then they filled it with water. This watery ditch was called a moat. Enemy soldiers got wet and cold if they attacked the castle from the moat. It was hard to fight from the bottom of it, too!

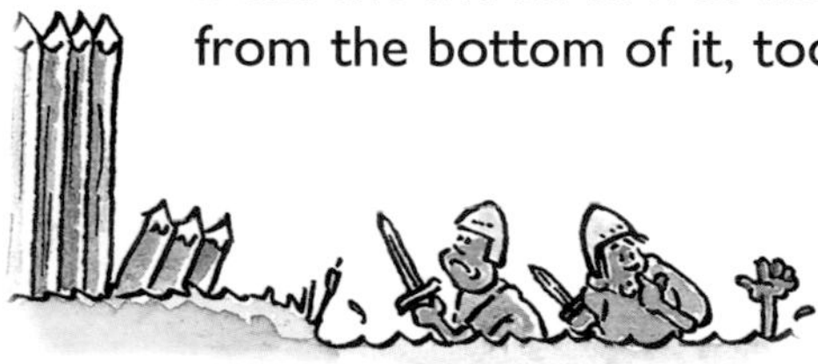

Think

Stone castles were a lot warmer in winter than wooden ones. Why do you think this was so?

What was inside the castle?

A big courtyard was inside the castle. This was called a bailey. A thick wall was built all around it. Smaller buildings were put up inside the bailey. Sometimes there were gardens. There were often animals and chickens, too!

Where was the safest place?

The safest place in the castle was a tall, strong tower. This tower was called a keep. The lord of the castle lived there with his family. In later times they slept on the top floor. There were big rooms downstairs to hold feasts for visitors.

Thick walls!

The walls of the keep were at least 3.5 metres thick! This meant that building a castle took a long time. It was also a very expensive job.

How did people get bread and water?

A castle often had its own mill and bakery. Many castles got water from a well. The well was dug inside the bailey. A massive wheel drew water up into the castle. Later castles had piped water with taps.

Measure

The keep walls were 3.5 metres thick. Use a tape measure to see how thick this is.

What happened at knight school?

A knight had to train for 14 years! First, he went to a lord's house when he was seven years old. There, he was taught how to ride and to shoot with a bow. Then he became a squire and was taught how to fight with a sword.

Count

A nobleman's son went to knight school when he was seven. He studied for 14 years. How old was he when he became a knight?

Who had the best horses?

Rich knights owned three horses. The heaviest horse was used for fighting and in tournaments. The quickest was used for long journeys. The third carried the bags!

Dying for love!

Jaufre Rudel was a French knight. He sent love letters to the beautiful Countess of Tripoli, although he had never seen her! When he finally met her he fell into her arms and died!

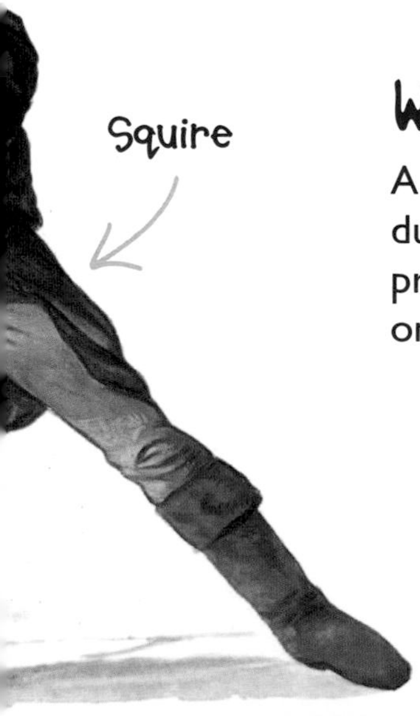

What was dubbing?

A new knight was given a special ceremony called a dubbing. First, he had to spend a whole night in church, praying on his knees. Then the new knight was tapped on the shoulder with a sword.

Did knights fight with a ball?

Knights hit the enemy with a spiked ball on a long chain. This was called a 'morning star'.

Knights used swords, too. Foot knights from Switzerland used a halberd. This was an axe with a hook on the back. It was good for getting a knight off his horse!

Get to the point!

Soldiers called 'retrievers' fetched all the fallen arrows. They had to run through the battle to get them!

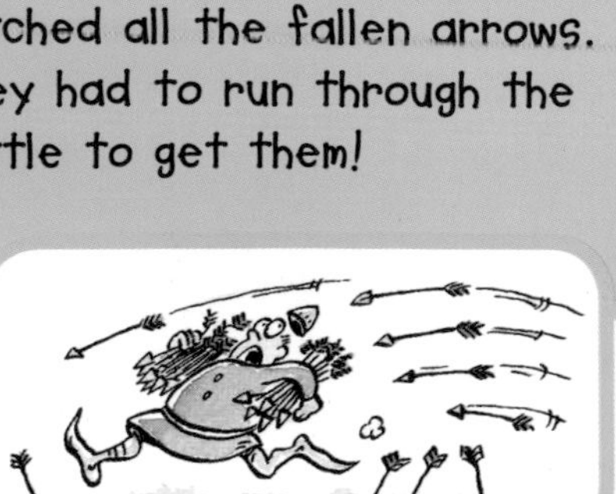

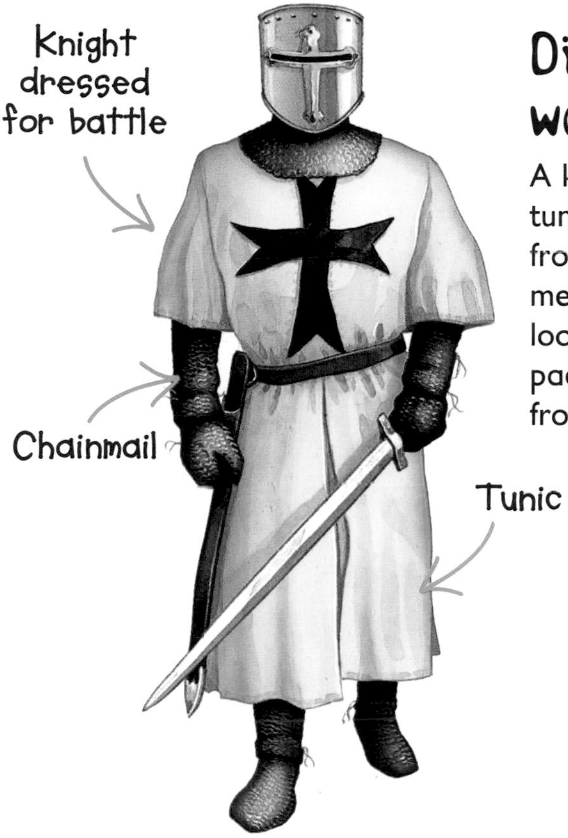

Did knights wear woolly jumpers?

A knight in early times wore a bright tunic with long sleeves. It was made from wool or linen. He also wore metal armour called chainmail. It looked and felt like knitted wire! A padded jacket stopped the chainmail from scratching the skin.

Design

In later times, knights wore steel armour. They even wore metal shoes! Design your own suit of armour to protect a knight.

How long was the Hundred Years War?

The Hundred Years War was fought between the English and the French. It actually lasted for 116 years, between 1337 and 1453. English and Welsh soldiers used longbows against the French. The bowmen could fire 12 arrows every minute!

How were knights told apart?

A knight wore a helmet that covered his head. Even his soldiers could not recognize him! Each knight put a special symbol on his shield and robes. The symbols and colours were called a 'coat of arms'.

Knight wearing coat of arms

Don't shoot the messenger!

Using a coat of arms was called 'heraldry'. This is because the lord's messenger was called a 'herald'. The herald wore his lord's coat of arms as he crossed the battlefield.

What was a herald?

A herald was a messenger. He carried messages for knights during battles. The herald had to be able to recognize each knight by his coat of arms. The heralds were very good at recognizing coats of arms. This eventually came to be known as heraldry.

Herald

Horse wearing coat of arms

Where did soldiers meet?

Each lord had a banner with his coat of arms on it. Knights and soldiers gathered around the banner on the battlefield. The lord could then explain his battle plans. The winner of a battle often stole the enemy's banner from him.

Make

Draw and cut out a shield from cardboard. Paint your own symbol on it.

Did knights have fun?

Yes they did! Knights took part in competitions called tournaments. These helped them to improve their fighting. The knights formed two teams that fought each other in pretend battles.

Did knights only fight on horseback?

At a tournament, knights also fought on the ground. They wore heavy armour. Skill and speed were much more important than strength.

Make

Write and design a programme for a tournament. You can include fighting competitions and entertainment.

Rotten cheat!

Some knights tried to cheat in a jousting competition. They wore special armour that was fixed to the horse's saddle!

Knight taking part in a tournament

How did knights find a wife?

Ladies from the king's court went to tournaments. The knights showed off their bravery to their favourite lady. Each knight tried to push another knight off his horse with a long pole called a lance. This was called jousting.

Jousting knight

What was a siege?

People sometimes became trapped inside a castle if the enemy surrounded it. This was called a siege. The people inside could not get food supplies. So they had a terrible choice. They could either starve to death or surrender to the enemy.

Think

Try to think of ways to get into a castle without being seen. Look at pictures of castles to help you. Draw a map of your route into a castle.

Battering ram

How did the castle crumble?

Sometimes the enemy bashed down the castle gates with battering rams. These were thick tree trunks capped with iron. The enemy also tried to climb the walls with giant ladders. Huge catapults hurled burning wood and stones.

Hairy weapons!

Giant catapults were wound up with ropes made of human hair! The hair was made into plaits and was very strong.

Siege

How did enemies get inside a castle?

Sometimes enemy soldiers dug tunnels underneath the castle. They then popped up inside the castle walls. The enemy also pushed wooden towers against the castle walls. Soldiers hiding in the towers leapt out and climbed into the castle.

Quiz time

Do you remember what you have read about knights and castles? These questions will test your memory. The pictures will help you. If you get stuck, read the pages again.

1. Why were castles built on hills?

page 310

2. What was a moat?

page 311

3. Where was the safest place?

page 313

4. What happened at knight school?

page 314

5. What was dubbing?

page 315

6. Did knights fight with a ball?

page 316

7. Did knights wear woolly jumpers?

page 317

8. How were knights told apart?

page 318

9. Where did soldiers meet?

page 319

10. Did knights only fight on horseback?

page 320

11. How did knights find a wife?

page 321

12. How did the castle crumble?

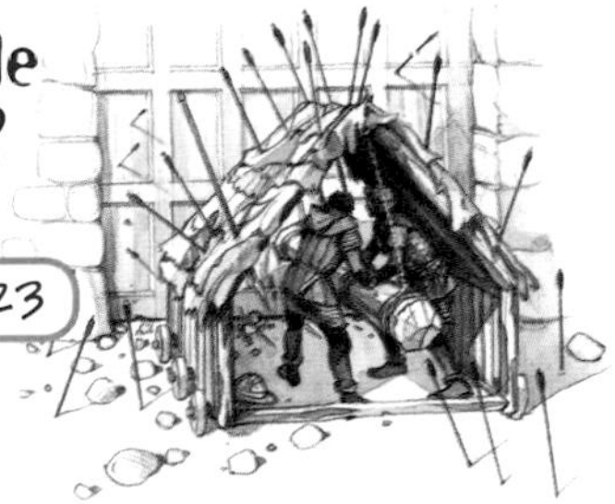

page 323

13. How did enemies get inside a castle?

page 323

Answers

1. So people could see the enemy
2. A watery ditch around a castle
3. The keep
4. Boys were trained to be knights
5. A special ceremony for a new knight
6. They fought with a spiked ball on a chain
7. No, they wore chainmail and tunics
8. By coats of arms
9. Around the banner on the battlefield
10. No, they also fought on the ground
11. When they were jousting
12. The walls were bashed with battering rams
13. They dug tunnels under the castle

Questions about...

Pirates

What is a pirate?

Pirates are people who steal from ships and ports. As soon as the first ships began to carry goods, pirates began to attack them. About 600 years ago, there were many pirates sailing on the seas and oceans around the world.

A pirate attack

Hairy pirates!

'Barbarossa' was a nickname for two pirate brothers. 'Barbarossa' means 'Redbeard' – because they both had red beards!

Who was afraid of the Barbarossas?

Every sailor was afraid of the two Barbarossa brothers! They were pirates who attacked ships about 500 years ago. One of the brothers captured the town of Algiers in North Africa. The other attacked ships that belonged to the Pope, who was the leader of the Christian church.

Make

Make your own Barbarossa mask. Draw your pirate's face on card. Use red wool to make a big red beard.

Did all pirates want treasure?

Pirates from the Mediterranean were called corsairs. They didn't want treasure. Instead, they took people from ships and ports and sold them as slaves. Corsairs also captured rich people. They were paid a lot of money to release them.

Corsairs and their ships

Who stole the Spanish gold?

About 500 years ago, Spanish captains sailed to the Americas. There they found gold, silver and jewels. The Spanish stole it from the American people and took it back to Spain. Pirates often attacked the Spanish ships before they got home and took the treasure from them.

Act

Try to act out your own story about Spanish and English captains. One is trying to steal treasure from the other.

When were pirates not pirates?

English captains such as John Hawkins raided Spanish treasure ships. England and Spain were enemies at this time, so the English thought it was okay to steal from the Spanish. The captains wanted to be called 'privateers' instead of 'pirates'.

Pirate queen!

Queen Elizabeth I of England encouraged her sea captains to be privateers. However, the privateers were often robbed before they reached England!

Can you be a pirate with one leg?

Yes! François Le Clerc was a dangerous pirate with just one leg. In the 1550s, he raided Caribbean islands owned by Spain. He captured the port of Havana on the island of Cuba. No one would pay Le Clerc to give up the port, so he burned it to the ground.

François Le Clerc

Did sailors fight the pirates?

Sailors fought hard against pirates when they were attacked.

But they didn't try to fight François L'Olonnais in the 1660s. He was very cruel and tortured his prisoners. When Françis attacked a ship, the captain and sailors usually gave up without a fight.

Captain surrendering

What did pirates do with their money?

Pirates sold their treasure to people at the docks. They usually made lots of money. Most of the money was spent in public houses!

Spend! Spend! Spend!

Pirates could spent 3000 pieces of silver in one night. That's about £45,000 in today's money!

Where was there a pirate paradise?

Port Royal was a harbour on the island of Jamaica. A strong fort guarded the harbour. Pirates could even mend their ships in the docks. Jamaica was ruled by the English, who left the pirates alone.

Paint

Paint a pirate scene with ships and a port. There might be lots of ships, with the pirates carrying their treasure onto dry land.

Pirates in Port Royal

Could women be pirates?

Yes, they could! Mary Read dressed up as a man and became a sailor in the 1700s. Her ship was raided by pirates and Mary decided to join them. Her ship was raided by 'Calico Jack' and his wife, Anne Bonney. Mary made friends with Anne and they fought against the navy.

Mary Read and Anne Bonney

Make

Make a plate of food for a pirate's prisoner! Take a paper plate and stick on cut-out food – such as caterpillars!

Whose prisoners ate caterpillars?

Ching Shih was a Chinese pirate. In 1807, she controlled many ships that raided China's coast. Ching Shih was a great leader. She had very strict rules for her sailors. Her prisoners had to cat caterpillars in boiled rice!

Ching Shih

Baldy!

Grace O'Malley shaved her head to look more like her sailors. She was given the nickname 'Baldy'!

Who said she was sorry?

Grace O'Malley went to sea when she was a young girl. She ended up controlling pirate ships off the coast of Ireland. Grace had 20 ships under her command. In 1593 Grace asked Queen Elizabeth I of England to forgive her for being a pirate.

What were the best ships?

Pirate ships had to be very fast! Many were small and easy to sail. Schooners were ships that had two masts. Corsairs sailed in galleys – ships that had oars as well as sails. The captain had a cabin in the stern (back of the ship). Treasure, gunpowder and food were stored in the hold, beneath the deck.

Where did pirates sleep?

Most pirates slept on the deck unless the weather was bad. Some put up hammocks below deck in the middle of the ship. It was cramped, smelly and noisy. This made some pirates ill. So did their food. They didn't eat enough fruit and vegetables!

Recycling!

Pirates even stole their prisoners' clothes! They usually sold them, but sometimes kept the best items for themselves.

Write

Look at the picture of the galley. Write a guided tour of the ship. Describe how the pirates lived on it, too.

What did pirates eat?

Pirates mostly ate dry biscuits and pickled meat when on board ship. They hunted for fresh meat when they landed on islands. They also collected fresh water and fruit. Pirate cooks often had only one arm or leg. They couldn't fight, so they cooked!

Who was afraid of a flag?

Merchant seamen were terrified when they saw the flag of a pirate ship. Early flags were bright red. By the 1700s, pirates flew black flags. Each pirate captain added his or her own symbol. Sometimes this was the famous white skull-and-crossbones.

Were buccaneers heroes?

Buccaneers were violent thieves. Some people thought they were heroes. Bartholomew Roberts was a buccaneer. His nickname was Black Bart. He was handsome and bold, yet he never drank anything stronger than tea! In the 1720s, he captured 400 ships.

Duck!

When pirates attacked a ship, they shot at sailors working on the sails. They also shot at the helm, the steering area of the ship.

Pirate flag

Where was the treasure?

Sailors often hid their treasure. Pirates had to break down walls and doors to find it. They threatened their prisoners until they revealed the treasure. Pirates had frightening weapons such as knives, daggers and pistols.

Pirates looking for treasure

Design

Design your own pirate flag. Choose a bold colour. You could draw your own frightening symbol on it.

What was the best treasure?

Gold and silver was the best pirate treasure. It could be gold or silver coins, plain bars or made into fine ornaments. Silk cloth and hardwoods such as ebony were also valuable. So was ivory. But pirates were not so happy with cotton, coal or iron.

Pirates and their stolen treasure

Spicy sands!

Spices from India and Sri Lanka were very valuable, but they were difficult to sell. Pirates often dumped them overboard. These spices piled up on the beaches.

Was the treasure shared?

The captain was in charge of sharing out the treasure. Officers got more than ordinary sailors. The cook and the carpenter got less because they didn't fight. Captains tried to divide everything fairly. Unhappy pirates might attack the captain and take over the ship!

Make

Make a mini treasure chest. Take a small box and paint it to look like wood. Then fill it with painted cut-out jewels.

Where were all the jewels?

Pirates stole jewels from ships all over the world. Diamonds came from Africa. Red rubies and blue sapphires came from Burma. Green emeralds were mined in Colombia. Divers scooped up shiny pearls from the Persian Gulf.

Treasure chest

What were pirates scared of?

Shipwreck was a pirate's greatest fear. Terrible storms could blow up in the warm waters around the Caribbean, the Indian Ocean and the Far East. In 1712, a storm blasted Port Royal in Jamaica. Winds smashed ships to pieces.

Shipwreck

How did pirates find their way?

Pirates used the position of the Sun and stars to guide them in the right direction. They also used a compass to help them. A telescope helped pirates to see landmarks and work out their position. Pirates used maps to find their way on land.

Write

Pretend you are captain of a pirate ship. Write down all the jobs that are carried out on board every day.

Round and round!

Captain William Dampier was a brilliant navigator. This means he knew where he was going! In the 1680s he sailed around the world three times.

How did pirates save a sinking ship?

Pirates tried to pump out water if the ship was leaking. Sometimes ships 'ran aground'. This means they got stuck in shallow water. The pirates had to throw out anything heavy. This helped the ship to refloat. Sometimes they threw out food barrels and cannons.

Who is Long John Silver?

Long John Silver is a one-legged pirate. But he isn't real! He appears in a book called *Treasure Island*. This adventure story is all about pirates and buried treasure. It was written by Robert Louis Stevenson in 1883.

Dancing pirates!

Blackbeard was a real and dangerous pirate. In 1798, his story was made into a ballet!

What ate Captain Hook's hand?

Captain Hook is a fierce pirate in a story called *Peter Pan*. It was written as a book and a play by J.M. Barrie in 1904. Peter Pan is the hero. He cut off Captain Hook's hand and fed it to a crocodile. That's why the Captain needed a hook.

Captain Hook

Did pirates sing?

Gilbert and Sullivan were famous songwriters. They wrote a musical about pirates in 1879, called *Pirates of Penzance*. But the pirates were softies! They wouldn't steal from orphans – children who had no parents – so everyone pretended to be an orphan!

Write

Write your own pirate story. Your pirates can be kind or cruel. They could be modern pirates. What would treasure be like today?

Quiz time

Do you remember what you have read about pirates?
These questions will test your memory. The pictures will help you. If you get stuck, read the pages again.

1. What is a pirate?

page 328

2. Who was afraid of the Barbarossas?

page 329

3. When were pirates not pirates?

page 331

4. Did sailors fight the pirates?

page 332

5. What did pirates do with their money?

page 332

6. Could women be pirates?

page 334

7. Whose prisoners ate caterpillars?

page 335

11. Where were all the jewels?

page 341

8. Where did pirates sleep?

page 336

12. How did pirates find their way?

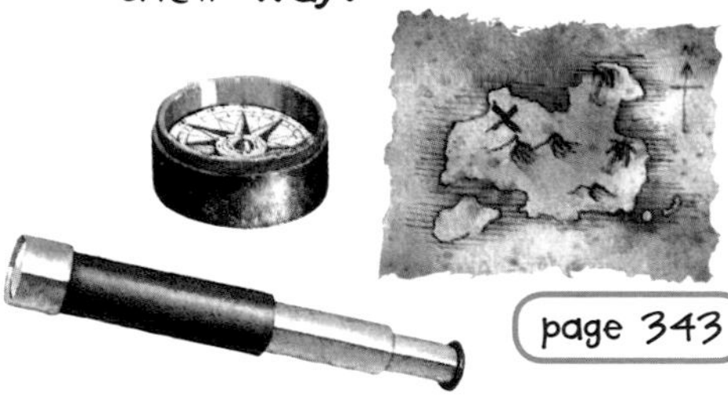

page 343

9. What did pirates eat?

page 337

13. What ate Captain Hook's hand?

page 345

page 338

10. Who was afraid of a flag?

Answers

1. A person who steals from ships and ports
2. All sailors
3. When they were privateers
4. Yes, sailors fought hard against pirates
5. They spent it in public houses
6. Yes, they could
7. Ching Shih's prisoners
8. On the deck, or below deck in hammocks
9. Dry biscuits and pickled meat
10. Merchant seamen
11. Jewels came from all over the world
12. With a compass, telescope and map
13. A crocodile

Questions about...

Explorers

Who was Marco Polo?

Marco Polo was a famous explorer who lived in Italy in the 1200s. He travelled to Asia at a time when most people in Europe never went far from their homes. Altogether, Marco travelled over 40,000 kilometres.

Marco Polo

Think

Imagine that you are a famous explorer. Write a list of everything you would need to take on your travels.

What did Marco Polo discover?

Marco Polo discovered lots of amazing inventions on his travels through Asia. He saw fireworks, paper money, ice-cream and eyeglasses for the first time. He also discovered that the Chinese had a postage system and could post each other letters.

Empty deserts!

On the way to China, Marco Polo crossed the vast, empty Desert of Lop, now called the Gobi Desert.

Who searched for a gold city?

In the 1500s, Spanish explorers searched for a mysterious city called El Dorado. Everything in the city was said to be made of gold. However, they never found the city, and people believed that the gold had been melted down and sent abroad.

Which explorer was very unlucky?

In the 1300s, Moroccan explorer Ibn Battuta, dreamt that a giant bird picked him up and carried him away. Battuta thought that the dream was a sign from God, telling him to go exploring. During his travels he did not have much luck. He was kept prisoner, chased by pirates, attacked by thieves and shipwrecked.

Why did explorers travel in junk?

A junk was a giant Chinese sailing ship. In ancient times, Zheng He, a Chinese explorer, had the largest sailing junks on Earth. The biggest was 130 metres long and 60 metres wide.

Discover

Where did you last go on holiday? How did you get there? How long did it take you?

Who was not allowed to explore?

Xuan-Zang, an ancient explorer, was banned from exploring by the Chinese emperor. He sneaked out of China and returned 16 years later with holy books and statues. The emperor was so pleased, he gave him a royal welcome.

Family values!

In many of the places Ibn Battuta visited, he got married. He had several wives and children in different parts of the world!

Who brought back a giraffe?

The Chinese sailor, Zheng He Zheng, was one of the world's best explorers. In the 1400s, he sailed to Africa. On his travels he collected precious stones, plants and animals to take back to the emperor. The emperor's favourite present was a giraffe from east Africa.

Zheng He Zheng

Star sailing!

Before the compass was invented, the first explorers had to rely on their observations of the Moon and stars to find their way.

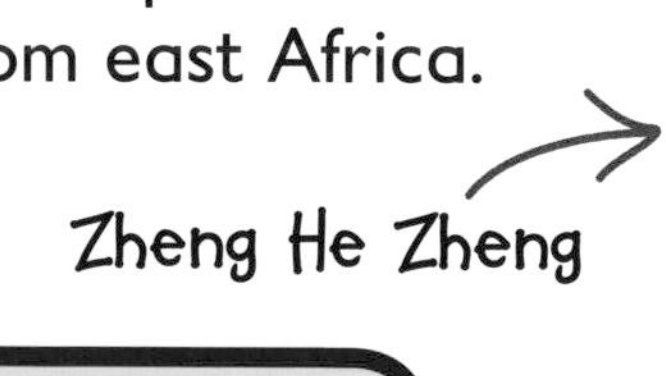

Discover

Can you name any spices? Do you know any foods that have spices in them?

Vasco da Gama

Who found the route to Asia?

In the 1400s, Portugese sailor Vasco da Gama sailed to Calicut in India to find spices. The rajah, Calicut's ruler, did not let da Gama take any spices, so he went home empty-handed. However, the King of Portugal was very happy that da Gama had found the sea route to Asia.

Why were spices like gold?

In the 1400s, spices such as cinnamon and nutmeg were as valuable as gold. Spices came from Asia and were carried to Europe on the backs of camels. This took a long time and made them very expensive to buy.

Who found the Americas?

Christopher Columbus found the Americas by mistake! He wanted to sail around the world to Asia in his ship the *Santa Maria*. When Columbus spotted land in 1492, he thought he had sailed to Japan. In fact, he had found the Bahamas, just off the American mainland.

Discover

Which sea is closest to where you live? Look in an atlas or on a map to find out.

Why did Columbus make a mistake?

Because he had travelled to the wrong place! As Columbus thought he had arrived in Asia, he called the lands he found the West Indies, and the people he met, Indians. They are still called this today – even though the West Indies are thousands of miles from India.

Hot stuff!

Sailors were afraid to sail around Africa. This was because of a myth that said if people went too far south in the Atlantic Ocean, the Sun would burn them to ashes.

Where was Vinland?

Five hundred years before Columbus, the Vikings found a new land and called it Vinland. They left after they kept getting into fights with the local people. Today, Vinland is known as America.

Who played a nasty trick?

The Spanish explorer Francisco Pizarro captured the Inca leader Atahuallpa in 1532. Atahuallpa said that if Pizarro set him free, he would give him a room filled with gold. Pizarro agreed. Once Atahuallpa had handed over the gold, Pizarro killed him and took over the Inca capital city, Cuzco.

Why did a dog get paid?

Spanish explorer Vasco Nuñez de Balboa sailed to America in 1500 looking for treasure. He took his beloved dog, Leoncico, with him. Leoncico never left his master's side and Balboa even paid him his own wage.

Whale of a time!

When sailing past Scotland, Greek explorer Pytheas was amazed to see fish as big as boats. In fact they weren't fish – they were whales.

Vasco Nuñez de Balboa

How did explorers tell the time?

Explorers could not tell the time at sea because clocks didn't work on ships. John Harrison, an inventor, created a new clock (called the chronometer) that could measure the time precisely, even at sea.

Look

Next time you go on a journey, write down how many different kinds of animals you see.

Which city was hiding?

In the 1400s, the Inca people of South America built a city called Machu Picchu on top of a mountain. Built from large stones and watered by a spring at the top of the mountain, the city was so well-hidden, that Spanish invaders never found it. An American explorer re-discovered the city in 1911.

Play

With your friends, play a game of hide and seek. Take it in turns to be the hider and the seeker.

Who founded the New World?

In 1607, 100 British people arrived in what is now called the United States of America. They founded the first permanent settlement and others soon followed. The continent was named the New World, and Europe, Asia and Africa became known as the Old World.

Ferdinand Magellan

Rich pickings!

In the 1500s, Francis Drake captured a Spanish treasure ship. It was carrying a cargo that was worth more than £12 million in today's money.

Who tried to sail around the world?

Portuguese explorer, Ferdinand Magellan, wanted to sail around the world during the 1500s. Magellan thought he could get to Asia and buy spices. Many of his crew died from a disease called scurvy and Magellan himself was killed in war. Only one of his five ships sailed home safely.

Who went on an important mission?

In 1768, Captain James Cook was sent on an important mission by the British navy. He went to the island of Tahiti and made observations of the planet Venus passing in front of the Sun. He also explored Australia, New Zealand and the Pacific Islands and made new maps.

What was scurvy?

Scurvy is a serious disease that is caused by not eating enough fresh fruit and vegetables. Many explorers and sailors suffered from the disease when on long voyages, as they had no access to fruit and vegetables.

Try it

How much fruit do you eat? You should eat five pieces of different fruit and vegetables every day to stay healthy.

Dr Livingstone

Captain Cook

Which explorer went missing?

In 1869, the explorer Dr Livingstone went missing. He'd gone exploring in east Africa and no one had heard from him. Everyone thought he had died. An American writer, Henry Stanley, found him in Tanzania. He greeted him with the words, "Dr Livingstone, I presume?"

Tasty trip!

Captain Cook was the first European to discover Hawaii, in 1778. He called it the Sandwich Island.

Who first crossed America?

Meriwether Lewis and William Clark travelled across America in 1803.

They sailed down rivers on a boat. When the rivers grew too narrow, Lewis and Clark used canoes. Local Native American guides helped them paddle their canoe and find their way across America.

Brotherly love!

Lewis and Clark met some fierce native warriors whilst exploring. By amazing chance, the warrior leader turned out to be the brother of their guide.

Rene Caillie

Who went exploring in disguise?

The French explorer Rene Caillie wanted to visit the ancient city of Timbuktu, but only Muslims were allowed in. He dressed up as an Arab trader and sneaked into the city in 1828. He was the first European to go there and return home alive.

Make it

Create a disguise for yourself using hats, sunglasses and old clothes. Does anyone recognize you?

Who was scared by bears?

American explorer Meriwether Lewis was chased by a bear whilst out hunting. Lewis tried to shoot the bear, but he ran out of bullets. The bear chased Lewis into a river, then walked away and left him alone.

Who tried to get to the North Pole?

Norwegian explorer, Fridtjof Nansen did. He built a ship called *Fram*, which was designed to get stuck in the ice without being damaged. It was the strongest wooden ship of its time. As the iced moved, it carried the *Fram* nearer to the North Pole. Nansen almost reached the Pole in 1895, but not quite.

Pole position!

In 1911, the explorer Roald Amundsen and his team were the first people to reach the South Pole.

Who crossed Australia?

The middle of Australia is so hot, it is very hard to travel across. In 1860, Robert Burke and William Wills entered a competition set by the government to cross the middle of Australia. Both explorers starved to death and only one member of their team survived.

Burke and Wills

The *Fram*

Who were the first Australians?

Aborigines were the first people to live in Australia. They arrived from Asia over 70,000 years ago. Many Aborigines lived in the Australian outback. Here, it is very hot and dry, and a long way from any big towns.

Discover

Write a list of all the different animals you would expect to find in Australia.

Did explorers travel by sled?

In 1910, an explorer called Roald Amundsen used dog sleds to travel to the South Pole. Husky dogs pulled the sleds, and if a dog died, it was fed to the other dogs. This reduced the amount of food the men had to carry. Amundsen reached the South Pole in 1911.

Who conquered Everest?

On 29 May, 1953, Tenzing and Hillary, were the first people to reach the top of Mount Everest, the highest mountain in the world. Since then, many other people have climbed the mountain.

Think

What sports can you play in the ice and snow? Have you tried doing any?

Peary and Henson

How did explorers keep warm at the North Pole?

By wearing sealskins! American explorer Robert Peary and his assistant Matthew Henson wore sealskin clothes when they travelled to the North Pole in 1909. The skins were light, waterproof and very warm. Peary paid local people to make his clothes and equipment.

A mountain of rubbish!

Today Mount Everest is covered in litter and old oxygen tanks left behind by climbers.

Who explored the natural world?

Charles Darwin went on a round-the-world voyage on a ship called the Beagle. Darwin was a nature expert and found many new birds, plants, insects and other living things. Once back in England, Darwin wrote important books about the natural world.

Charles Darwin

Who discovered nine cities?

In 1870, a German called Heinrich Schliemann travelled to Turkey to see if he could find the ancient city of Troy. He discovered the ruins of nine cities, and also dug up piles of beautiful gold jewellery.

Going ape!

In 1871, Darwin wrote a book called *The Descent of Man.* In the book, Darwin said that the very first humans were related to apes.

Which ship explored the seabed?

In 1872, a ship called HMS *Challenger* set out to explore a new world – the bottom of the sea. The ship measured the seabed, using ropes to find out the depth of the ocean. On its round-the-world voyage, *Challenger's* crew also found many new kinds of sea creatures.

HMS *Challenger*

Draw

You have discovered a new type animal. Draw a picture of it and give it a name.

How did people get to the Moon?

In 1969, astronauts travelled to the Moon in a spacecraft called *Apollo 11*. It was launched into space by a huge rocket. It took three days to get to the Moon. Once there, the astronauts spent two hours exploring before flying back to Earth.

Apollo 11

Look

Can you see the Moon and stars when you look at the night sky?

Space animals!

The first astronaut in space wasn't a human, but a dog named Laika. Sadly, Laika died during the voyage, but she led the way for more space exploration.

Who was the first man on the Moon?

The first person to stand on the Moon's surface was American astronaut Neil Armstrong, followed by Buzz Aldrin. They were part of the crew of *Apollo 11*. Both men collected rocks to take back to Earth.

Yuri Gagarin

Who was the first human in space?

In 1961, Yuri Gagarin became the first human to go into space. Gagarin flew around the Earth once in his spacecraft called *Vostok 1*. This took nearly two hours. He then travelled back to Earth and landed safely.

Quiz time

Do you remember what you have read about explorers? These questions will test your memory. The pictures will help you. If you get stuck, read the pages again.

page 351

1. Who searched for a gold city?

page 352

2. Which explorer was very unlucky?

3. Who brought back a giraffe?

page 354

4. Why were spices like gold?

page 355

5. Who played a nasty trick?

page 358

6. How did explorers tell the time?

page 359

page 362

7. Who went on an important mission?

8. Who was scared by bears?

page 365

9. Who tried to get to the North Pole?

page 366

10. Who were the first Australians?

page 367

11. Who conquered Everest?

page 369

12. Who explored the natural world?

page 370

page 373

13. Who was the first man on the Moon?

Answers

1. Spanish explorers
2. Ibn Battuta
3. Zheng He Zheng
4. Because they were very valuable
5. The Spanish explorer Francisco Pizarro
6. Using a chronometer
7. Captain James Cook
8. Meriwether Lewis
9. Fridtjof Nansen
10. The Aborigines
11. Tenzing and Hillary
12. Charles Darwin
13. Neil Armstrong

Index

Page numbers in **bold** refer to whole chapters.

D

E

F

G

H

I

J

K

L

M